HOME IS WHERE THE MIC IS

Edited by
Mandi Poefficient Vundla
and Allan Kolski Horwitz

Published by
Botsotso
Box 30952
Braamfontein
2017

botsotso@artslink.co.za
www.botsotso.org.za

ISBN: 978-0-9814205-4-7

We would like to thank the National Arts Council of South
Africa for its assistance in funding this book.

an agency of the
Department of Arts and Culture

Cover, layout and graphics: Chimurengalab

Photograph credits:
Pg 50 (Richard "Quaz" Roodt) - Still Skill
Pg 82 (Vangile Gantsho) - Matete Motsoaledi
Pg 108 (Vuyelwa Maluleka) - WordNSound
Pg 134 (Lexicon [Lex La Foy]) - Tainted Lens Photography
Pg 178 (Afurakan) - WordNSound
Pg 182 (Mandi Poefficient Vundla) - Philani Hadebe

FOREWORDS

For the last three years South Africa's poetry scene has seen a rebirth of poetry with young writers redefining the art form to better suit their lived experiences. This anthology ' Home Is Where The Mic Is' is the first collection of contemporary youth poetry that manages to fully capture the spirit of Spoken Word in a country as diverse and ever-changing as this.

Readers are given a unique view into the poetry of today, 20 years into a tricky and sometimes elusive democracy. Young writers are showing great courage in telling their stories in the most visceral of ways. Poetry stages have become interesting showcase spaces where poetry meets performance as well as a range of art forms. It is important though to strip the poet of his performance and the props, leaving just him and the weight of his words.

Delve into the world of contemporary South African poetry with Afurakan's hard hitting 'Blues For Madiba', Ewok's thought provoking 'Garden Boy? Kitchen Girl?' and Sarah Godsell quietly stirring 'Building'. Explore the wonders of a new-found sexual liberation and identity through Modise Sekgothe's 'Cunnilingus' and fall in love again with Ysra Daley Ward's 'Sthandwa Sami'.

South Africa has grown to be recognised as a must for travelling poets. Our local stages have played host to the likes of Yrsa Daley-Ward (UK), Luka Lesson (Aus) and Clint Smith (US). If anything, their work has shown that storytelling is an integral part of the human condition and that though we have oceans separating us their stories still hit home.

Qakhaza Mthembu

--OO--

How can you expect me to go back to the shadows?
Masai

*"REALITY IS A CLICHE FROM WHICH WE ESCAPE
BY METAPHOR"*
Wallace Stevens

*Poetry is born of painful awareness, created for an
immense minority, and is naturally averse to the swell
of conformity from every age. It requires unadorned
explosions of expression, channels of air blossoming
with sounds, the orchestras of the mind playing as a
single instrument, breaths overlapping and interlocking
like feathers on a wing, the body in thrall, surrendering
to the primitive contral force of the imagination.*
Keith Flynn

In the beginning was the Body; and the Body gave Voice to the Word; and the Word separated Silence from Sound, Noise from Music. And the Voice as it shaped Word gave substance to quietly versed Thoughts, raging Shouts, frenzied Pleas and tender Supplications.

Over the past sixty years the Spoken Word movement (in the guise of blues, beat, rap, hip hop and slam) re-energized the Written Word; saved it from obscure intellectualism, from excessive concentration on the eye (as page) and from pedantry as 'linguistic waffle'. For the Spoken Word, with bold gesture and subtle inflections of tone and lilt, has restored flesh to the Word and enabled a renaissance of interest in poetry, particularly by young people. This physicality and emotional force started as a North American/Carribbean movement but is now stimulating new forms all over the world. Here in South Africa it is a national movement with each major city having a number of regular platforms where Spoken Word artists can present their work at festivals, slam competitions, open mic sessions and workshops.

Moreover, though the North American/Carribbean styles and themes are still very much in evidence, more and more localized, indigenous ones are emerging. As we explore our own lives seriously, so we live them more fully, and recognize their significance. However much the Black American diaspora feels it is descended from the continent of Africa, its culture is still too absorbed in an urban ghetto/island struggle of a particular kind in relation to the "White world" to fully reflect independent African societies. Of course, the struggle in post-Apartheid South Africa has similar challenges but with Black Africans being a large majority there are important differences that call for different vehicles.

The current Spoken Word scene has several notable features. Firstly, there is the astounding way in which the English language is being used, particularly by those for whom it is a second language. Secondly, there is the richness of performance styles, ranging from the 'talking hand' to the strut, to the dance. Presenting a poem as a theatre piece enables the poet to inhabit a character, exhibit personality and amplify emotion – aspects that the written page alone cannot easily achieve. Another noteworthy aspect is the high participation of women who are bringing their own issues and styles and their own vocal patterns and musicality.

Lastly, one is struck by the intellectual quality as well as mastery of form that so many of the poems embody. There is real weight in the explorations of identity, of history, of social and economic relations, of sexual politics, of generational ties, of the vocation to make art. With regard to form and rhythm, though rhyming (and the rhyming couplet) came to be seen as outmoded in European and North American poetry, the African (diasporan and continental) Spoken Word has reinstated this form and injected an amazing new vitality. Having said this, the many forms/rhythms given expression in this anthology show that poets are as comfortable working in free verse as they are in rhyme.

In short, the oft ventured criticism levelled by South African academic critics that performance poetry is a crude 'upstart' that dilutes the intellectual and linguistic rigour of our poetic tradition is simply unfounded. Such criticism constitutes a continuation of the establishment's rejection of much of the poetry that in the 1970's and 80's took on an openly political, agitational stance. In this case, the Apartheid nature of our society played a major role in devaluing the Spoken Word. As someone who has tried to write and present various types and styles of poetry I can say with confidence that there is no contradiction, and that there is, in fact, no competition. The two are complementary and should be viewed as brother and sister in the same family.

All told, the twenty-four poets captured between these covers should give you a more than passing taste of what the Spoken Word movement in our country (plus a few 'foreign' friends'!) is generating. After reading their work, the next step, of course, is to catch them in action – the social media and arts websites will give you directions. Be prepared for a powerful experience that will add immeasurably to their read words.

Allan Kolski Horwitz

7

CONTENTS

TUMELO KHOZA

Tumelo is a Spoken Word artist from Durban. Her style fits in the Performance Poetry category. She is not afraid of speaking the truth where politics are concerned, being very vocal about how the people find themselves tricked and victimized by the system, if ever, and how, at times, they are helped by the system and acknowledging how far society has come with regards to mending what was once a difficult era. She also writes about matters of the heart, society, gender differences and equality, exploring the different shades and colours of the language by means of figures of speech and imagery.

DEMOCRACY

There's a teenage boy/ who presently chills at the corner/ where the future intersects with our history/ his name is Democracy/ he's forever mumbling what sounds like poetry/ forever high on a spliff of our dis(joint)ed society/ forever sniffs on the stiff aroma of whiskey/ counting how many governing bodies make the front page daily.

He seems forever tipsy/ everybody thinks he is crazy/ when actually/ he is only a reflection of you/ and me/ raggedy/ fashionably styled with the finest fouls of humanity/ compliments of our parliamentary authorities/ who lift a clenched fist of a revolutionary hypocrisy!

He spits in prophesies/ expresses his powerful mentality/ but nobody wants to listen to him carefully/ too obsessed with the honey of money that sting the BEEs/ it's no wonder our flag is forever asking Y endlessly

He reckons it's probably the immorality of society/ that these policies work only for the ones with big bellies/ who embrace the inheritance of polygamy/ who stand behind podiums publically and speak proudly of their deeds/ while our country is falling apart at the seams/ who are forever power-hungry/ driving our state to calamity/ strategically holding strikes an rallies/ that fuel the youth with doom and catastrophe.

Forget what happens in the rural vicinity/ forget that they do without electricity/ and unless they travel to rivers of hope/ with leaking buckets of broken homes/ they will be thirsty/ forget they are currently suffering from our currency/ with a vocabulary that amounts to nothing more than the abbreviations of political parties/ AIDS and HIV/ forget they are constantly promised unity but are forever fed the contrary/ see/ such leaves Democracy angry/ it leaves him tearing his book of rhymes in fury/ because no one wants to listen to him as he speaks whole-heartedly/ so Democracy lights a ciggie and chills by his corner silently with his container of gasoline/ he folds his country flag neatly/ slowly takes a drag/ pours the gas/ lights another match and utters, "Phuck this man!"

tunnel of self reflection, become the god we seek

there are lost ones among us, who utter the same language we speak

bare, they tread upon this earth as corpses

every breath has a price tag, especially when hurt endorses

they fly, kill the sky with their winglessness

a heart that is beat feeds on hopelessness

i am fatigued by their carelessness

i am only a spirit passing through this life and through all these humans

all these humans have deserts in their eyes

and nothing in their lives

where i come from, we dance

our mouths are the goblet in which gold is spoken and meaning enhanced

rainbows reign from our tongues

we do not feel lost, on our shoulders is where our souls are hung

and we walk,

even though we understand that we are here in passing

we talk

even though we understand that here is not where we will find ourselves dying

only if we give in to what they believe in will we lose ourselves

and unless we refrain from losing ourselves

will we know

that there is more to the sun that is forever rising

because the horizon is limited by our third eye

and only if it sees beyond the invisible line of infinity

will we have so much experience through this flesh we have been captured in

the net that caught us,

on the vast ocean of self in our mother's womb

at times her umbilical cord is a noose
the passage way that paves an escape
and often i see light in that direction
when the walls cave in

in case you see blanks on our faces, know that we
are hidden within –

our smiles will support the self-forgotten
the ones who compromise their being in order to
rise from the bottom
we will remind them that they are more

we will remind them of the greater cause

here, we are sun flowers
we bow to the moon
and give praise to the sun
we embrace the monsoon
and can admit when we are undone.

i wish they could see what we see.

When You Dance
Your body becomes an inferno
So much fire in your soul
Fueled by the spirit that is
the channel for the ancient
Meandering through your bag of
In search for secrets

When you dance,
The Earth knows it needs to shak
It knows to reverberate the anthems
of your & tapestry
Stories of warriors and martyrs
Whose remains come alive
When you allow the drum of your
heart to beat faster

When you dance,
Your anatomy speaks it's own langua
A translation of tribal cave-written Scrip
Bare feet, wild lair and leads
The kind of rhythm
that will have

BLACK PADDED BRA

Yesterday I wore a black padded bra
That matched my white hot pants
With black lace at the trim
And I felt so sexy!
Like I had ten thousand men just staring at me
Yet none had the ability to touch me.

I stared deeply at the woman in the mirror,
Her eyes swung on an imaginary pole,
Her body ripe with fertility and silk –
She slithered from this pole of longing,
Brown and red as the sunset,
She knew what it meant to be an object
And to reject the laws of one's temple.

She imagined herself soaring across the universe,
Bending her body backwards to God's breath.
Naked as the wind,
She laced her feet like a pattern,
Stood there,
Planted in the ground
With no purpose and raging desires,
Motionless and beautiful
With the make-up of replaceable masks on her face.
The scars on her face are only the surface of the
gashes in her soul,
But still, she smiles,

Like a blossoming flower
Grown from an oak-tree at the top of the hill,
With blood dripping from her lips
And a heart ripped and torn apart.
But still, she smiles, regardless,
Reminding her soul that a God exists somewhere
In her broken heartbeat –

He
Finds rhythm in each breath she inhales,
Irrespective of whether she has herself draped
In a black padded bra
And matching white hot pants
With black lace at the trim!

She's sexy,
But daydreams of purple
Blush across her cheeks.
A destroyed identity.
All she sees is the silhouette of her figure:
Naked and shapeless in every form.

Tell her she is beautiful.
Tell her that the dirt she had on the surface of
her skin
Has blown away like powder from her smudged
mascara.

Tell her that within her weakness
are the traces of her power

And all she needs to do is focus on the
greener grass
Outside the shut windows of her mind,

Because she can!

And the rusted chains that she sees in the mirror
aren't really there!
So she has nothing to worry about.
It's ok to cry,
It's ok to break,
The rain will water the cracks
and flowers will grow there one day!

She should just go with the flow,
and stare back at the mirror,
and see me standing in front of her,
wearing a black padded bra,
with matching white hot pants,
with black lace at the trim
and feeling so sexy!

WHEN YOU DANCE

Your body becomes an inferno
So much fire in your soul
Fueled by the spirit that is song,
the channel for the ancient
Meandering through your bag of bones
In search for secrets

When you dance,
The Earth knows it needs to shake
It knows to reverberate the anthems of
your tapestry
Stories of warriors and martyrs
whose remains come alive
when you allow the drum of your heart
to beat harder

When you dance,
Your anatomy speaks its own language
A translation of tribal cave-written
scriptures
Bare feet, wild hair and beads
The kind of rhythm
that will have you tongue tied when you
speak

Dikson has been performing spoken word since 2006 when his virgin outing saw him qualify as the youngest competitor in the semi-finals of the UK-wide BBC Radio 4 poetry slam. Now based in Zimbabwe the artist has organised festival events, worked with youth on varied projects and performed across Europe and Southern Africa. His poetry has been translated into German and Danish and he has featured on radio in South Africa, Zimbabwe and the UK. He has been part of jazz-fusion acts, electronic and poetic fusions and is part of the global poetry and jazz fusion group, Sonic Slam Chorus. He is currently the workshops, conferences and exhibitions manager for Zimbabwe's fastest growing international festival, Shoko. The focus of the festival is on empowering urban youth and culture by providing a platform for urban art forms and artists. He is also the editor and creative director of the Zimbabwean youth platform, Kalabash. The website was launched in May 2013 and has become the country's leading youth opinion site.

DIKSON

COUSINS FROM THE PAST

We tailor relationships out of Velcro, guts and gelatine
It sets awkwardly, a warm mess housed in a crunchy static fabric
The crackle when it rips clawing at liquid cords of thread
The needle pierces our finger's skin and leaves blisters so the blind can read the Braille of our miscarriages and regrets
We are not qualified to weave and stitch
We are science projects that ooze orange custard lava when we're not supposed to
Our anger is just frustration with a voice when we don't see eye to eye

We carried this trade on from our elders, dressmakers and gentleman's outfitters, butcher's of cloth with good intentions
Who would have thought that a song title as shitty as 'forever young' would ring so true if you read it right
Our ancestors are just our cousins from the past, who needed floats when they were swimming and stabilizers on their bikes to ride

They waded through this just as we are, and maybe they could share some wisdom but I don't believe in oracles
Their grudges sewed the future so that none of us were born naked, but clothed within their rigid laws and draped in their decisions

We fall in love and melt through each other's cracks like goo in a broken fortune cookie and hope our choice reads right
We play it by ear, the same way we always have, on any continent, no matter what was in fashion at the time or how the buildings were constructed or which conqueror had more slaves to drive
Sometimes we get possessed and dress images on our lover's backs, we knit quilts to cover whole nations and religions in stereotypes
Grownups playing grown up need to remember just how small they are and how vast is their lack of knowledge

We never learn from our mistakes just perpetuate the fumblings of our cousins from the past

If I asked you what home was I wonder what you would say

Because home for me is the small dusty hand-print on the inside of white-washed walls

The calling card of a child who knows that life lives just outside, halfway between the doorway and the sky

It's the way that half sun softens and shows universal languages of selflessness when it wraps crimson textures on red soil before she sleeps

Under a moon the beams silver spoons vivid, so alive, you'd imagine cats in cradles, bovine astronauts and check your dish for legs

If you get my gist just listen, it's harder than it sounds

Home is the way that plants grow through holes in the road to the way that time means everything and nothing depending on whether you're using a clock or your tongue to tell it

Because two hands aren't big enough to measure its depth, you're my presence, your past or direction

It's making plans off beaten tracks, it's the fact that where I'm from there's a traffic light that shows red and green at the same time like reflections of life are enshrined by crossroads

But we live on a sphere where people like boxes and lines that define where home begins and ends like we weren't built to share gardens that shelter what's yours and mine

Like our sunshine is eclipsed by difference

Its cloaking skins in Union Jacks, Zimbabwe Birds and Star-Spangled Banners that make us forget the true meaning of a human home

We can still hold hands over a dead man's depiction of a bordered world

And my story isn't written on one page

So home for me is also passionate rebellion in the underbelly of an imperial beast

Its activists branded with tipsy dreams of freedom for all

Malfunctioning cogs in a man-made machine that's always been operated under the influence of the most corrupting of drugs

It's having the power to blow clouds away with cigarette smoke because you don't know how cold it sometimes gets

Home for me is warmth

If it's places for you then for me it's people whose bric-a-
brac bricks break down walls and make this place seem that
little bit more open

Because I want to believe in

Japanese Rastafaris with Bolivian roots and Palestinian Samurais with a penchant for change

Zimbabwean Ninjas seeking scrolls 'cos they can, Swiss Anarchists who make mocolate for fun

Poachers who pedal the skins of their
counterparts just to make a point,
commercial rappers who believe their 'crib'
is not their home

And Roman Emperors who act like
Buddhists when in Rome.

Home for me is knowing that borders are
scabs

Dried up bloodlines of kith and kin

Conqueror and slave

Flags in a dust that moulds all footprints
and praises no leader or tribe

A dust that has no warring desires,

Humble enough to colour feet regardless of
skin

To make horizons you could cry to

Not lines in the sky

It sees itself as the canvas on which the longing
we have for one another finds paint

To make art that looks like Rockabilly, Dubstep,
Reggae/Jazz Fusion spat in Creole Hip Hop

With a cappella breaks on silent nights styled by
a Euro-Tech Dread-Punk to flickers of a banjo,
birimbau and a chorus of stirring string and horn
sections

A dust

That will touch paw prints of children to leave
us memories of a younger wisdom that screamed
out

With unclenched fist

That home is only ever as far away as the
distance between me

And everyone you've ever known

And you.

CARNIVAL

I imagine they swayed at the shore

Digging heels into sand like birds to seed

Hands overflowing with stones like the faces of demolished city markets

Fingers and streets keeping secrets

Civilisations entrenched in palm lines like combat wounds

Bones flesh deep & clenching like pillars slow dancing to the snake charmer's flute

Nails and knuckles blush white like slow burning lanterns in a sunless sky

While lips part and close in a single movement as the wind's dictionary measures the length of your breath

In silent unison raising fists sunflower petals unfurl to skim stone and seed across oceans for infinity

Touch continents and minds until carnivals of colour explode in both

Kaleidoscopes shattering shades of yellow, black and green, through loud speakers like Trenchtown party poppers weaving through the traffic of sound waves

Beats bursting through plumes of curried goat scented smoke

Aba shanti-i guarding vinyl's like Bilbo Baggins in a dread cap

That's roots rock reggae blaring through bass bins convulsing weight spewing bombs onto concrete, crushing cans in its wake

Feet stomp, crowds mouth the call of timeless vocal chords bouncing histories through mega & microphones

Speaking the language of a moving mass of people draped in summer's finest sun and warmest dimpled smiles

Ribcages pulsating to good vibrations like the sound was intravenous or injected into skeletons

Turning suburbs into dancehalls and pavements into shorelines until backstreets become private parties for the public to enjoy

Reclaiming common ground if only for a day, its soundtrack seeping through the gaps between tower blocks and narrow minds like floodgates were a flip-switch

And grannies learnt to whine again, ripping covers out of judged books and peeling back the years

Children start to move like notes were written in the crowds

Cops and robbers hustle through baton thrusts and nervous glances, night embraces silence putting fingers to the lips of the loudest people's party

Groups disperse like cluster bombs into parks and illegal raves, shrapnel in the city breathes, walks in slurs and chuckles to the punchlines of a day

We'll sleep again like middle-aged school mates hungry for reunion

With whistles round our necks and islands in our eyes we'll play make believe to samba bands and party revolution

I STAND

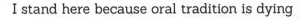

I stand here because oral tradition is dying

And because we don't tell stories around fires anymore

I stand here because I want you to see the ventricles hanging from my symbolism

Like Daily Mail readers clinging to life by the threads of their cynicism

I want to give you licks with a mallet made of tongues

They say a picture tells a thousand stories, and one day I want to give a thousand brushstrokes to one…

I stand here because talking to strangers is far from dangerous

You've been helping me find my way home as far back as I can remember

Ask me for directions and all I can tell you is the roads I've been down and the ones that made my feet bleed, the ones that made me nervous and the ones that gave me sweet dreams

I stand here as a listener to the potholes when these streets speak.

I stand here with a half-smile and a blood-stained roadmap wrapped in a skin that's almost see through

With a past of clogged arteries and a future of broken veins

I stand here as an ode to broken poems

Wandering around the inky blueprints of what soon will be a home.

I stand here because second-hand crucifixes weigh too heavy for this heathen

I stand here because a storyteller got turned into a reason

Not to value life but make it death that we believe in.

I stand here because we've been playing human pyramids for so long

It's like the people at the top have forgotten what it feels like to be down to earth so they've busied themselves with games

Like trying to catch the sun while we talk to the moon about her role in darker days.

I stand here because misinformation she's a damsel with no decency

She put poison in the water and her daughter's courting industry

If you wish to read on please turn to page 3 where she

The woman inside her

Is more than just a pair of breasts just like sunset is more than just a backdrop for skyscrapers.

I stand here because there's nothing wrong with telling you that you're beautiful

And if you want to hug a tree go find yourself a forest because you're a damn sight less crazy

than naked emperors jacking off to genocide and if you fail to understand me my friend we're flying in different skies.

I stand here because I miss bedtime stories.

I stand here because oral tradition is dying and because we don't tell stories around fires anymore.

I stand here because I want you to see the ventricles hanging from my symbolism

Like Daily Mail readers clinging to life by the threads of their cynicism

I want to give you licks with a mallet made of tongues

They say a picture tells a thousand stories and one day I want to give a thousand brushstrokes to one...

TERESKA RENÉ MUSHOND

Writer, poet, performing artist, social and cultural activist, Tereska began cultivating her mastery of the arts as a tender six year old thespian destined for the stage. She went on to study Drama and Theatre Art at the University of the Free State in her hometown Bloemfontein. During this time she also underwent extensive dance training at the Performing Arts Council of the Free State (PACOFS). She drew from her experiences as well as her writing skills and theatrical aptitude to create the collective !Bushwomen, a performance art ensemble that combines poetry, song and dance to address social ills. Due to the success that !Bushwomen experienced Tereska was recognised on national broadcasts media like 3Talk, Weekend Live, Kwela, numerous radio interview slots and on the print media as a voice for many without a voice. She has been a scriptwriter for etv's popular daily drama, Scandal and is currently writing for a children's programme on SABC, Inside the Baobab Tree. While studying towards her Honours degree in Creative Writing at the University of Witwatersrand she is also wearing the hat of playwright for her second play entitled Te Veel Vir 'n Coloured Girl, which won Best Debut Production at the Vryfees Festival in Bloemfontein.

MOONLIGHT

Moonlight is the name of the mortal

that transported my sombre mind

from its cage

to the planes of Drakensberg mountains

From nowhere he appeared

Silently made his presence felt

Our brief encounter leaving me

yearning for more

Moonlight is the name transcripted on
my index page

Page 289 – the last page

But when turning to that page you'll find
it blank

Moonlight is a mystery

My mystery

His beautiful ebony skin gleaming with
a twinge of twilight blue

The way he looked at me

Makes me want to make him do things
to me

His strong black hands touching – no –
feeling me

Feeling my unwanted feelings

My distorted thoughts

My unspoken words

No middle name

No last

Simply…

Moonlight

NOTE TO MY SISTER

You are beautiful
enough.
Your hair is
enough.
Your Angolan in-laws
who sponsor your Brazilian hair
do not know
enough
to know
you are
enough
for us.

Tell your mother-in-law
Sorry, please tell your mother-in-law
my mother says
she must stop taking you for manicures.
Those Korean nails are not strong
enough
to hold
enough
of you
and us.

SOMETHING

Something happens
To you
When you are woken up
By angry voices
In the cold silence
Of night

Something happens
To your brittle body
When you know
Something is about to happen
To your mommy
In the room
Next door

Something whispers
To you
To cover your baby sister's ears
So she can sleep soundly
And continue her dreams of angels and fairies

Some things break
Inside you
When you hear the beat
Beat

Beating
Of his fists
On her fragile flesh

Something tears
You apart
As you rush
To her side
In the morning
After he has gone
Her purple eye
From her swollen face
Unable to meet your dilated pupils

Some Thing forces
You to your knees
Where you pray
Beg
Bargain
With God
For the terror
To stop

And it does

Something happens   angry
When you are woken up by ~~surprised~~ voices
In the middle of the night

Something happens
~~As~~ And your body starts to ~~strive~~ To your brittle little body
When you know
Something is about to happen
To your mommy in the room next door

Something ~~tells you~~ whispers to you
To cover your baby sister's ears
So she can [sleep soundly]
And continue her jovial [~~dream~~ dreams of angels & fairies]

Something breaks inside of you
When you hear the beat, beat, beating
                              fragile
Of his fists on her ^flesh

Some things choke you into ~~a silence~~
Muffling the screams

          ~~Fear~~ rushes
Something ~~pulls~~ you to her bed
Her purple eye from her swollen face   rooms in the ~~morning~~ morning
Unable to ~~look again in the face~~ meet your dilated pupils

Some THING forces you to your knees
Where you ~~look out at God~~ pray, beg & bargain with
~~Pleading~~ for the terror to stop

Something
Somewhere
Somehow
Sometimes
Anything

But just when you think
It was but a fleeting nightmare
The walls whisper to you
Telling you
The quiet is too quiet

Sshhh…
Listen…
Look…

Curtains neatly hanging
Fence freshly painted
In the garden children playing
Passers-by admiring

The dance of deception
The deception of the dance
The waiting for the terror
The terror is the waiting

For something
To happen
On a day just like today
When some thing
Explodes in his head
And you feel the fear
In his footsteps

Something jolts
You to the spot
Taking you back to
The familiarity of the original fear

Something dies
In your spirit
Making you bleed
Before the bang
Bang
Banging
Of her head
Against the wailing walls

Then something happens
You grow up
You forgive

But when night falls
And all are asleep
You cry
For that something
That happened
To that little girl
Who is still waiting
For some thing
To happen
To make her forget

MASAI DABULA

Born in Johannesburg Masai Mululeko Dabula is a writer, poet, photographer, art entrepreneur, journalist and inventor. Having been raised by struggle veterans he sees art as a weapon to interrogate youth apathy towards their status quo and inspire change. From this, a thriving career in art as activism was sparked, seeing Dabula creating artistic movements that have since 2005 given voice to aspiring performers. Dabula's poetry has previously been published in an anthology called 'Grounds Ear' (2011).

HOW CAN YOU EXPECT ME TO GO BACK TO THE SHADOWS?

When time, has consumed my soul making it dark, skin too thin to hide in myself, thoughts too loud to be killed by silence.

I've collected all my broken dreams to make yet another pillow to rest weary shoulders, belief has left me hollow, and I'm tired of playing hide and seek with things that lurk in the dark forcing me to know the mind of God.

I've seen hell bound angels who forgot how to fly, earth bound demons who deny the fact that all must die.

I've watched my mother hide her fears in his name, pray her sins and wage away. In those cold parish chairs pray to see tomorrow whilst her life passes her by.

How can you expect me to go back and kneel in the shadows?

We are angels that forgot how to fly, wings too black and beautiful to be caged in these matchboxes for home.

We know the tongue, we speak to the land. We know where our roots lie buried; our blood echoes with the rhythm of the land. I am not going back to the shadows, to pledge my legions to a foreign God whose servants can't even pronounce my name. I'm not going back to the shadows, to kneel in that thick silence hoping that answers to my suffering will slip through the open slits of my leaking roof.

You will not bully me back to the shadows, shadows have no choice but to follow the subject, hence we are all subjected to fulfil your order, all around me are borders I cannot cross just of the darker shade of my skin, the tongue that I speak and burdens that my forefathers left me with. I know what darkness means, I am still grieving the unjust death of my people, weeping and pleading freedom to stop killing my people.

I will not go back to the shadows.

People living in a hole feast on each other to survive, wear thick skin that only death can peel off, they feed on each other's tears.

I am not going back there, swallowing my pride cannot be my staple meal.

Being poor remains my people's crime and the scraps you pay me cannot make up the bail to free my life from these chambers. Disease has started to quench us out of our lives, patience making worms meat out of our bodies, these bodies that are vacant temples that no God could live in

I AM FIVE

No one ever speaks to me about my father; they tell me my grandmother is my mother. My mother, my sister; I am that child no one ever speaks about, that child who brought shame to a house that failed to house itself.

I am seven.

I start questioning heaven, for my grandma is spending most of her time in taverns. At times I wish my step-grandfather was still with us. It's been years since he left, yet the scars he left on grandma's face always reminded me why we had to move from shelter to shacks, rundown flats in Hillbrow seeking refuge from his wrath.

I am seven and a half.

I realise it's my birthday, I am all alone, I was born alone. I wish for a cake, but all I have is flickering candle light on a three legged table pushed to the corner to disguise the missing leg, white noise from a black and white TV set plugged into a car battery for power and drunkards banging against our shack as they try to make their way to the core of that stinking skwatta camp called Dunusa.

I am nine.

I am now a man, my mother came back with another baby brother, I can make his bottle and I can feed him. My back is his transport to crèche, his clothes sometimes mine to wash, I watch him grow as my own.

I am eleven.

I don't need my father but we need the money, for I fear being hungry. I am starving for any kind of attention. I miss my mother's perfume, I miss her scent but I need my grandma to be fine, she's the only person I have. Her drinking habit is giving birth to other habits and I refuse to love her to death.

I am thirteen.

I don't care, I start sagging my pants, I have been shagging my bed and I am dating that beautiful woman from my wet dreams. My erection is stronger than my attention span; I'm a fan of Real Man. The streets have fathered my perception. Gained survival skills from observing, I too dream of speeding and spinning cars. I want to shoot till I became one with the gang of stars.

(In her name)
The stars are out
tonight, care to moon
walk with me dear
Azania? The bags
beneath my eyes
carries stories of
hope.

(Time)
The skin is beginning
to fold, hold me,
for we are getting
old.

(Mastery)
I know how to turn
her bruises to
a fine jazz tune.

33

I am fifteen.

Now I have to fit in, no need for sitting indoors when you can be climbing high walls, picking locks or breaking doors. Corners have taught me that all women are hoes, bent over, both hands on that stale beer-reeking tavern toilet seat. I didn't know that I too could become one. Broken and confused, the pats of my friends on my back sew back my ego and my reputation went from zero to hero.

I am seventeen.

"I remember, yes I remember but I was high and tipsy. I don't remember what happened to the condom."

Whilst my peers worried about acne, I am worried about finding more innovative ways of hiding my baby's aching stomach. My baby was carrying my child, fathered by a child who struggled to fit in his father's small shoes. Fear crippled me, relocation proved to be the only solution, yet my love for her made my knees far too weak, her heart was mine to keep.

I am nineteen.

I do not know what love is but I know what love isn't. I cannot stop her from leaving; I'm tired of pleading with her to stay. My pockets do not go deep enough to satisfy her desire, I'm too poor to afford what she's growing to admire.

I wish I was fifteen, no I wish I was six, no I wish I was never born. I am given more than I can take; I need to redefine my fate. It seems like God has made me bait to lure and catch the Devil, I'm becoming a proper slave, and I know I have debts to pay for the mistakes I've made yet looking for a job is a job that I struggle to afford. I now know that a person's worth is weightless compared to their wealth.

I am twenty-one.

I now know that I can never leave anything to chance, my past cannot determine my destiny and I know my life like the back of my hand. Over the years, books have taught me how to stop begging and start demanding what is rightfully ours. My history is a stage of broken plays.

But love taught me to forgive and let live, forget and let my scars do the talking without pride.

I am twenty-five.

And I meet you; I can't imagine life without you.

With you I can remember the future like it was yesterday, yet no one is special.

I SOMETIMES SLUMBER

I sometimes slumber on the thoughts of my shadow and watch my widowed memories weep for their lost entity, waking up before dawn and staring at my window, watching the sun as it tears the blanket of the night bringing a stiff light that slowly alters to rays that feel like millions of needles on my skin.

My face turns darker as the day gets brighter and I realise that space doesn't create a place, a place doesn't create a house, and a house doesn't create a home.

My thoughts continue to mock me, I decide to close my eyes and watch my eye lids opening my heart like the door to let the orphaned wind in.

What I feel has a life of its own, it troubles me more than it puzzles me, concludes me more than it confuses me, and heals me more than it touches me.

She's a sweet disorder; she's the light I once held in my palms. I fall from her sight, but her nights are owned by a mere man who doesn't see the beauty in his careless hands.

MTHUNZIKAZI A. MBUNGWANA

Mthunzikazi Mbungwana otherwise known as "NolaliwaseCala" is a poet and a social commentator from a small village of Cala in the former Transkei. Her inspiration lies in cultural activism and a need for the betterment of lives of the forgotten areas, formerly known as homelands. Through her poetry, Nolali promotes, embraces and celebrates cultural diversity and uses the power of the spoken word as part of the solution. She believes that the role of a poet is to provide a mirror for society to reflect and track the various journeys all its components are engaged in. She now lives in Midrand, Gauteng where she works as a public servant.

A SONG FOR DUMILE FENI

It must be sung in low key
But not too soft and not with haunting keys
There will be no burning of white candles
And women in heavy, black regalia
Because here we are not mourning

This is a song for Dumile Feni
It won't be belted out of the well-layered stomach
Of a mezzo soprano
The goose-bumps might cage us
Make us weak

The song won't be of up-tempo beats
This is no time for celebration
Silently the rubbish man infiltrated our spaces
Although we can't remember his face
His broken soul that yearned for warmth
Is visible unavoidable in his ash drawn portraits
He told the stories of the neglected majority
Their names will never hang on street poles

This is a song for my son, our son
Zwelidumile Mgxaji
He cocooned himself
Under the name Dumile Feni
Zwelidumile, the world heard him and lamented
His country rejected him, reduced his art
And his pulse to rubbish
They suffocated him to death
Silently the rubbish man sketched his heart out
The west dragged him silently and exploited his talents
To glorify themselves as messiahs of the black man
From poverty stricken Africa
The same Africa whose resources they looted
After making her children slaves
Feeding them lukewarm food
That didn't flatter the palate

03 March 2012

~~The truth~~ ~~truth~~

~~Maybe if~~ The truth

If I were to cut off my tounge

Lend you my ears

~~Would you be Courageous enough to tell the truth~~

Would you tell me the truth?

Nhunzikazi Oblas

Who is Dumile Feni?

No one knows

Who cares?

No one cared to listen

They were busy feeding the ones

Ready to be slaughtered

They forgot to water the plants of the future

Into blossoming black lilies that would never wither

He exited quietly
No one noticed

Over the thousand hills

He continued to express himself

Foreigners heard him

Or at least they pretended to hear him

They claimed his fortune

Shone on his shine

This is a song for Dumile Feni

A lonely boy who became a man

A man ahead of his time

A man who was brave enough

To search for understanding

For the link between death and birth

Religion, spirituality and fantasy

Evil and good

Dumile Feni kept on sketching

Oblivious to the ticking clock

The setting and rising of the sun

As his father had prophesied at birth

And said, Zwelidumile

Only after his cardiac arrest

After his death

Did this nation hail his name

As one of us.

Ifikelele kwesisimo,
Kuchithek' ilindle,
lwabolisa yonke indawo
ungagxeka bani ke ngokufa kwebhokhwe
isezwa iyeza?

Ubungekhe usijul'entlango
wakugqiqba usirhalisele ngamathontsana amanzi
Uwuhluphezile umbundlwana,
ngoku yingqeqe edlavuza,
amaqath' endwendwe
Lo mzi awungeni bantu
Thula ukhalelani?

Liphalale igazi labantwana babantu
bengenatyala
Ziqungqulizile iizidumbu, bafa njengezinja
Abafazi bakhala isijwili emva kocango
Amadoda ayangqukuleka enkundleni,
Abantwanana bayazidlalela emva kwezindlu,
Bejong' enkalweni becula besithi,
Utata uyezangomso, uzakusiphathela izibiliboco,
Zase Marikana, Marikana-Marikana!

What's that cry?
Marikana 16 August 2012

The arrival of time was announced
Not by a ticking clock but a rattling barrel,
Emptied bowels rotting the hilltop, subdued cries and
tattered apparel
What could we do with our trembling hands up in surrender?

The monster master threw us into the desert
Only to tempt us with tongue-wetting little water drops
But the throat remains dry and sore.
The pup you provoked is now a raging bull dog
Barking at passers-by and biting at visitors' heels
Soon the sores will be septic and never heal
No one shall enter this home, not while wounded dogs snarl
But why the shock, why the cry?

Clotting blood splatters the hill rocks, we cry
Wounded bodies of the innocent strewn, brothers lay dying
A young newly-wed gives a heart-wrenching cry from
under the veil
Screaming a loud grief-prayer to gods and God
While little children unknowingly play their after-rain songs
"Daddy will bring me gifts from Marikana,
Marikana, Marikana!"

ABANTWANA

Ababuyanga abantwana,
namhl' ilanga litshone emini,
inja nganye izikhotha amanxeba

Ababuyanga abantwana,
Akukho mntu uyinokozayo,
Yindaba yakwamkhozi
Imandlalwana yabo ilalelwe livukazi,
phaya ngasegoqweni

Abatshakazi bawuphekile, bawuphothula,
bawuphaka umqa kungoku nje,
ugcwele iintanda

Akabuyanga amadodana entabeni,
You see in my culture women are not allowed to
talk about these things,
It has been thirty nine days since my brother
went up the mountain.

Children

The sun sets at noon
Dogs lift their legs and lick their wounds
The children have not returned from the mountain.

Fathers gather around shaking heads
No one shall say a word,
But the little bundles of dirtied blankets say it all
A dried blood stain says a thousand painful words

The maidens have prepared a feast
Only to throw the calabashes to dogs and pigs
There will be no feast and there will be no funeral
There will be no coming-home celebratory ululations
But moans and sobs of grief as we silently mourn
The non-return of boys that were nearly men

Menfolk will not talk about it; mothers cannot dare
mention their names
In hushed tones they give cold condolences
"It's culture" they say, and look away

The children will not come back from the mountain
They lay in shallow graves, unmarked
We shall never see them, or their graves.

NGUMNTAN'OMNTU

Wamzala seliyokutshona ilanga,

wambeka entendeni yesandla sakhe,

wamfahla inkaba ngothando, ububele ,
nokuzithemba

She gave birth at dusk
To a bouncing beautiful bundle of joy
Confidently the umbilical cord was cut, carefully, heart full of love

Wakhula ekrelekrele enxanelwe ulwazi, nemfundo

waphumela ngaphandle elizweni,

elimqengqelezi

bamqoba amadolo, bamnyelisa bembiza
amagama,

nabo bebefanelwe kukumkhusela,

abo baqhayisa ngokuba ngamakholwa,

bamnukuneza.

A giggling toddler grew into bright teenage mind
Hungry for words, yearning for the Message
She went out to slippery slopes of the World
To deliver that message of Love and compassion
But the world forced its own message
Of revulsion, revolt and ridicule
Supposed protectors leading the attacks
Religious and righteous throwing the first stones
The abuse went unabated and unrebuked

Kwathamba amadolo,

wamngcikiva umvandedwa,

isono sakhe sinye qha, kukuthanda,

lo uthandwa yintliziyo yakhe.

With resolve weakened and dream deferred
She felt isolated, despised and betrayed
The supposed guilt led to a harsh sentence of hate
Locked in cold cells of queer languages
Rape called corrective, murder called phobia
Her only sin? To love the one in her heart.

* Translations to English: Thembelani Ngenelwa

SARAH
CATERPILLARWINGS
GODSELL

Sarah is a poet and a historian. She has grown up in Jo'burg and has a deep love for this city. She began performing in 2009 and has since appeared on a number of platforms, the first being Poetry Delight and co-hosted the music & poetry evenings 'Freshly Sliced', intimate conversations with women through poetry and music in 'The Kats Kum out to Play' as well as having participated in Jozi House of Poetry, Sanaa Africa 2013 and 1000 People Boogy. Her work has been published by Botsotso online and she contributed to the first artistic response to the Marikana massacre: 'Marikana, an anthology', published by Geko in 2013.

BUILDING

We are building on
Spiderwebs

But it is working.

Slowly, slowly
Step only this way, careful
Careful
This one falls
That one falls

But we are
Slowly
Slowly
Rising

We are building on
Volcanoes
Here

Round the bubbles
And sink holes
Careful here, this
Ground looks stable but it's
Just crust, really, building on
red hot
Red hot

We all get burnt
Battle-scars painting songs on
Our faces

But it's working
Slowly
Slowly
We are rising

We are building on ghosts
Here,
Comrades
Careful of this one's
Face,
That one's mouth.

We need to understand
What they need now,

To build them into our
Bricks like graffiti
So they can still sing
So they can still scream
And we cannot forget

So we can see them clearly
And lay flowers before them and
Not pretend. Not pretend.

Because this one fell
And that one fell
(and tears, tears fell)

But we are building.
We are building.

hammerkop

I collected toes
Yours mine hers, hung then in
The flesh melted off
Hammerkop grabbed the bones
Us, intertwined in his nest.

IN THE MIDDLE OF US

We were waters
You rapids
Me oceans
Making our way to some other sea

Feeling our rocks we mixed
Chaotically
Moments of peace thrown up
To the moon
Spray screams calmed by the flow

As we flowed the water ways
became
Less and less clear
Silt and soil collecting
beneath us
The faster we flowed

We came to a tree
In the middle of us
I went round and
You went round and
We expected to meet each other
On the other side

But we never found each other again

The river changed path while you
Stopped to taste the trees roots

And i ran on towards a sea
The tides
Changed and the moon
Now holds us apart

Your spray pushed you out
Of the water and you grew
New legs
New ears that
Didn't hear my water wailing

I swallow your tears
Because we can no longer touch

SMILESLEEP

I am trying to
Undo
Years
So I can sleep
For one moment
In your smile

PARIS IN THE SPRINGTIME

Cold bite in the air
sun coming out to play
mid day

air full of new flowers
new scents
but there is nothing easy about spring

each tree represents a triumph
hard fought
against cold and death and hard
emptiness
each blossom that makes it
is a prayer to that renewal
and an ache
reminding of that fight

don't smile
so easily at the spring, then
each blossom tree is also a battlefield

Richard 'Quaz' Roodt is a published writer, performance poet, writing coach and social activist from Johannesburg. Renowned for his passionate performances, he facilitates a non-academic creative writing class at the University of Johannesburg and is also involved in numerous poetry and social outreach programs around the country. In 2009 Quaz published his first collection of poems entitled 'The Orange Book: Vol 2'. He is currently working on his second collection due for publishing in 2014. He is the co-founder of the Johannesburg poetry collective 'Likwid' and has released three mixtapes and an EP and numerous other instrumental projects under his 'Sam English' alias. He also features on numerous albums, short films and documentaries.

RICHARD 'QUAZ' ROODT

DRUGS KILL FEAR

The sand man has gone fishing

Alone

I go hunting for sleep

Eyelids descend inviting darkness

Shadows reach for me

Sweat oozes

Wrestling with blankets

Uneasy in my own skin

The crickets won't shut up

Moonlight tears through split curtains

Blinding me

The tap drips, so I think

Digital clock warns:

Morning approaches like a lioness eying a tired deer

Sleep has abandoned me . . .

The crickets won't shut up

Maybe a book

Or a chat with the T.V

Or rather

Some Xanax and Donormyl

This, unlike last night, will really be the last time.

Becoming

Dancing alone
To the music of shadows
Something dead rots
away inside him

The music stops
He sits quietly
Enduring the stench
He knows...

Tomorrow flowers
will blossom.

QUAZ. ROODT

...AND ON THE 5TH DAY

Half awake

Drowning in a cup of black coffee.

The hour glass lays broken,

Time escapes and becomes forever.

The poet clothes his brittle soul in autumn leaves

Predicting winter for supper.

I have lost faith in tomorrow.

We live our feeble lives in the constant now

And right now, you are not here.

Alone,

My sharpened pencil speaks bluntly

Cuts violently into a virgin page

Chaining my loneliness to a company of poems

I tear away pieces of my wailing self

Preparing for life without you

And then . . .

Half awake

Staring at the coffee stains and your name

Etched into my wooden table

My heart smiles

As your distinctive voice tickles my waiting ear

From the other side of the door an announcement:

My cat has returned from his walkabout.

A HEART I BROKE

In the corners of my darkest self
I go searching for the light
Still my mood paints the day morbid
Murky waters lure me closer to
A wet end for this dry life
My tears become one with the lake

Our fairytale died
And with it my smile
The singing birds in my voice have
Gone silent
I explode into a swarm of bats
And claim the night sky
A dark mood for a once happy child
My unforgiving heart beats curses and spells
A cauldron of revenge for
A life wrapped in hate

I will see you again lover
And it will be the last time.

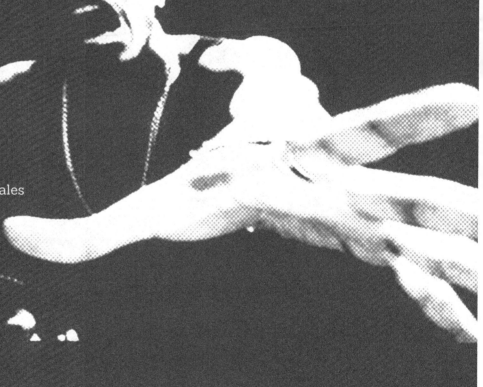

JAGGED

Swimming through shadows
I break the surface
Gasp and inhale the light
A lonely swimmer
Freestyling through murky waters
Violent storms slam my body
Against jagged rocks
Tearing away at my weak flesh

Spat out by this ocean
Amongst the skeletal remains of whales
And mermaids.
I found myself
Here I will heal and wait for you.

55

Yrsa Daley-Ward is a London based model, actor and writer of mixed West Indian and West African heritage. Born to a Jamaican mother and a Nigerian father, Yrsa was raised by her grandparents in the small town of Chorley in the north of England. She performs poetry in the UK and internationally, fusing it with theatre, music and storytelling.

YRSA DALEY-WARD

POETRY

Nobody is saying anything at the dinner table tonight

because everyone is too angry.

The only noise is the clinking of fine silver on bone china

and the sound of other people's children playing outside

but this…will give you poetry.

There is no knife in the kitchen sharp enough to cut the tension

and your grandmother's hands are shaking.

The meat and yam sticks in your throat

and you do not dare even to whisper, please pass the salt,

but this will give you poetry.

Your father is breathing out of his mouth,

he is set to beat the sparkle out of you tonight

for reasons he isn't even sure of himself yet.

You will come away sore and with an aching heart

but this will give you poetry.

The bruising will shatter into black and blue diamonds

that you will use to make your smile bright and your eyes shine.

Nobody will sit by you in class.

You will find a twin heart like yours, scarred a little,

maybe it will work most likely it won't the first time but that

will bring you poetry.

Broken trust will crumble into gold dust and maybe, just maybe,

you can grow from this

and this will open the door.

STHANDWA SAMI

In the early hours of this morning it was far too hot for anyone to sleep.

You told me I was strange and kissed me

sunk your teeth into my soft bottom lip

twice. So hard I thought you drew blood.

I keep getting the scary feeling that if you look at me for long enough you may see that I have a thousand fears

just like your mother who never really wanted you to leave.

Meanwhile mina I am catching up on the sleep that we missed

and waiting patiently to feel normal again.

My thoughts about you are frightening but precise.

There is no knife in the kitchen sharp enough to cut the tension and your grandmothers hands are shaking. The meat and yam sticks in your throat and you do not dare even to ask "Please pass the salt".

But this will give you poetry

I can see the house on the hill where we make our own vegetables out back

and drink warm wine out of jam jars

and sing songs in the kitchen until the sun comes up.

Wena you make me feel like myself

again. Myself before I knew any solid reasons to be afraid.

Last night you give me the space to dream bigger than the single bed

and brighter than the morning.

Your father is breathing out of his mouth. He is set to beat the sparkle out of you tonight for reasons he isnt sure of himself yet You will come away sore and with an aching heart but this will give you poetry

The bruising will shatter into black and blue diamonds that you will use to make your smile bright and your eyes shine. Nobody will sit beside you in class. You will find a twin heart like yours, scarred a little.

You laughed in your sleep and I cried in mine

and this afternoon we might be tired because the sun is fierce today

and too much happened between midnight and now

but bhabha, you are terrifying and brilliant so

I am the kind of woman who is already teaching my body to miss yours

without craving.

I am the type of woman who is teaching my heart to miss yours without failing.

And I am quite sure that you will find this unnecessary

but I am already searching for a place to run to and hide when you say,

"Uthando lwami. I'm ready. Are you?"

You know that I would gladly drive with you to the other side of the world with only the clothes I am wearing

and the loose change and empty peanut shells in my purse

kodwa every time you leave the room I worry

and think that perhaps I have imagined you.

Or maybe you have imagined me.

A FINE, AWFUL ART

You may have learned from your mother

or any other hunted woman.

Smiling at devils is a useful

learned thing.

Swallowing discomfort down in spades.

Holding it tight in your belly.

Ageing on the inside only.

Keeping it forever sexy.

I MISS YOU

I miss you in tiny earthquakes.

In little underground explosions.

My soil is a hot disaster.

Home is burning.

You're a lost thing.

THE SITUATION

she says she cries over me on the train to and from work

and one day it will be better but it isn't better now.

she is just like my mother, but alive.

knows how to love

quietly, completely.

something about the way a black woman holds your heart.

you can leave them all you like but you can't stay gone.

THANDO FUZE

Thando is a Durban based poet who has amassed the total respect of the poetry industry in the country. A member of a KZN super collective called 'A Sonnet of Poets', she continuously redefines herself and Durban poetry with her words. On stage Thando is a hypnotic performer. Her 'chilled out' persona, coupled with arguably the most impressive word collection, forces the listener to sit down and take it all in. In describing her work, Thando says, "It's nothing but life – its beauty and uncertainties".

OUR CITIZENS

There are citizens who get by and those who can buy.

They sleep belly full yet still growl, sleep easy yet wake up to nightmares.

They can afford but they owe attention too much. They speak of change but walk backward, have enough but ask for more, fat but eat some more.

All brain never gets it all if any at all it's true.

Ask the guy on that street corner playing a flute for coins, food for thought and even for the tummy, a fruit they never drop these citizens.

Walking on top of the world, top of the food chain with heavy chains dragging their hearts, less than kind smiles plastered across their faces yet they speak of reverence, inside screaming fuck benevolence.

They are planting trees that bear thorns, eating peas with a fork.

But you should see these kids that dig through garbage for at least that smell of KFC to trick the mind or at least that taste of ANC to feast on.

I blame the 'wise guys' that buy us with small change for no change.

Feeding us vocabs we don't get, calling us fools behind our backs.

These success keys are hidden in the machines, it's apparent, rape is a mission made possible

by pistols and 'piss tools' yet peace we still seek.

The youth is still sick, falling victim to life's ills.

Miss, treating AIDS, but still dies. School kids skip school for booze, 'cool kids'.

We have swallowed silence for way too long, it's time to regurgitate.

Let's educate each other and meditate on the truth.

Some of these citizens have a nerve to tell us to shape up or ship out.

We were never shipped if anything, we shaped this place to what it is.

Slavery eradicated? Really?

Bullshit! In the bundus we still use it to polish our floors.

Our flaws are bare for the world to see and mock us, used for mock-ups
to present overseas

yet none of us oversee these slide shows.

This shows how much we need to modify here, unify peers.

Yes, here, pressure mounts and covers us.

Blowing up our starved tummies, teen mommies of babies never born and
it's a trend.

Yes, here we abort kids, to hell with innocence, kid, we are from the
struggle,

we form the puzzle, reformed this jungle.

We hunt the hunters dry, bar tenders squeeze guitar strings to identify what we need to quench our savanna thirst.

Obsessed with the idea of being told 'you are free BEEs', yes, BEEs you are free, like swarms.

Slums are buzzing like pests annoying the hell out of government wanting to crush us citizens.

They are feeding us poisonous isms with the aim of killing us in our sleep.

Eyes wide shut we keep sipping. Skipping on fine lies, we'll forever seek and never find

because here there are no spoons, here there are no platters and silver is only found on the clouds.

Wake up! You've been dreaming for far too long.

STALKING STREET LIGHTS

A ton of also clipped our wings for some foolish reasons.

We were caught attempting to fly wingless, ignorance taking over our minds silently;

The nature of truth is that it always resurfaces at the sight of light into our king-domes

leaving folly hung at the edge of our sharpened tongues.

We forget about our five senses and get stuck in the centre of fear and disbelief

chaining our train of thoughts onto high school desks, we left behind bars of conformity.

I still dream of eternity, perhaps as a Sunday dish served on lazy afternoons resting my bones

on the bosoms of nature's grandchild, a seedling of misbehaving apple trees.

And, yes, I miss my grandmother sometimes, when she'd carve smiles onto my eyes.

She was a comforting grey cloud that never rained but bore silver linings where her teeth used to be . . . pretty.

I'm sure she still believes we haven't touched our wings, and whispers, "Nurture your halo" in your mother's ear before she makes you a cup of coffee because sometimes we can't cope.

We miss our wings.

I-believe-I-can-fly tattooed on our chests, superheroes suffocating inside us.

I still remember the dreams that left me breathless freefalling from the rooftop of hope,

growth grabbing me by the throat and a little voice saying,

"Find your purpose in these trying times and you might find your wings

on the rough edges of your carelessness."

Only reminded by our lovers breathing heaven on our necks, dreary, wearing beaded branded t-shirts

but we never worry about how our manners are dressed.

You find others addressing us in loose belts of arrogance, others in high heels of misdirection

relying on people magazine for an ounce of self-worth but our true worth isn't on these bloody carry bags.

DAY AND NIGHT

The sun thinks the moon has it easy.

The lights are summoned and when they bid goodnight, the night comes out to play.

But, before it can even show off, it falls, face flat on the floor beaten by the lies that come into play

and the plot thickens.

The deeds that take place sicken.

Mothers are out in the night cradled in the arms of men who aren't really men

but truly merge the terms 'boy' and 'turmoil' and mould these into one man

who cheats and chills in marked territory regardless of clear bands that shine.

Dancing in the night to Euphonic in our ears sounding distorted for we failed phonic at base phases.

We opted to fornicate in our teen ages, teens, they age early.

Let creased faces kiss the night while age
runs up to catch us.

Let us lift up barely developed tits for they
are our tickets to manhood;

after all Hollywood is just a dream we gave
up on chasing.

We were too quick to make up face, we
forgot we had minds that needed to be made
up,

to soak up elderly teaching but at night.

These kids, they seek elderly touches.

Hands with visible wrinkles silently ticking,
silently talking of wives left behind in houses

that barely have warmth, places you could
never call home.

They feed on hope.

They put their trust in the arms of night to
find comfort from the moon.

At night these men seek kids hopeless with
immature touches of palms that scream
'Mother'.

Eyes that twinkle in the night sky while
nursery rhymes still jingle upon the crisp lips

of under-age-lady-wanna-be's.

The voices inside us still believe that they
are the light we seek where the tunnel ends.

MPHO KHOSI

Born on the 11th of July 1982, a product of Wattville in Benoni where he started school and discovered his love for poetry, Mpho co-published a poetry and art anthology "Portraits of Propaganda" with Frank Lekwana as a test to see if the two could self-publish. In 2011, after a five year break, he returned to poetry and put his words to the test on the Word N Sound stage where he emerged as one of the top ten performers with poems such as "Encounter with Love" and "I refuse"; these would also appear in his anthology 'QUIETLYloud' published in the same year. He also performed at the first Word N Sound festival and thereafter at festivals in Swaziland, Pretoria and Durban. He was recently invited to be part of the Read-a-thon and Literacy Celebration week hosted by the Ekurhuleni library and is a mentor for up-and-coming poets from Westonaria high Schools. He has also been a part of DoGoodInc which assists communities by donating books and other reading material.

EK BEDOEL ME OM TE KLA ME

Ek bedoel nie om te kla nie,

Maar julle begin nou om julleself soos kaffirs te dra.

Dit is soos ons voorheen gesê het.

All you good for

Is to drink, dance and make noise,

Marry many wives, have sex and make lots of kids.

Just look at yourselves,

You have brought to life our prophecy;

Ons het mos gesê,

You cannot rule yourselves,

You are a symbol of poverty,

The bottom feeders of humanity,

Creatures of opportunity,

Like the rats that run riot in your townships,

You would rather step over each other to get what you want

Than work together to build what you need.

You are a disgrace of a race,

Lazy, mentally inferior people.

Truth is; allowing you to rule,

Is like letting the monkeys run the zoo,

But you are even worse than animals.

Ruthless, you rape your own young,

And abuse your own women.

Just look at what you have done to our once beautiful Johannesburg,

You have prostituted with her,

And now she stands as a squatter camp,

A refuge to pimps, druglords and net my Here weet.

She has become a waste land,

Even the faeces on her streets bears witness to that.

Then you wonder why we didn't want you to procreate,

Your offspring are monsters like the seeds from which they fell,

Constantly high,

Just to try and forget that their mothers were whores,

Their fathers, drunkards.

You see,

You are only tools to be used like a spade,

Useless without your master's guiding hand.

But your leaders,

Julle luiers was studente van ons,

They have learnt well from their masters,

And now they themselves have become monsters,

The art of instilling fear they have mastered,

Having seen what we did in Sophiatown,

They send in "Red Ants" to come and tear your homes down,

And with these so-called "Maberete"

They seem to slowly be implementing a curfew now.

Then to soften you up,

They throw food parcels at your doors.

And also remind you how they won freedom for you.

Places to educate, they will never build,

But shebeens and churches pop up at every street and every neighbourhood.

All they would rather do is indoctrinate you and keep you drunk,

Unbeknown to them,

They simply carry on our legacy.

Why should they create a breed of "clever blacks"

While you serve them well as their puppets.

Black pride, my foot.

I am being sincere in saying,

This is no complaint,

Maar julle begin nou om julle selfs soos kaffirs te dra.

EK BEL
MAR, JULLE BEGIN
TE DRA
DIT IS SOOS ONS VOORHEEN GESE
ALL YOU ARE GOOD FOR
IS TO DRINK, DANCE AND MAKE
MARRY MANY WIVES, HAVE SEX AND
JUST LOOK AT YOURSELVES,
YOU HAVE BROUGHT TO LIFE OUR
ONS HET MOS GESE "YOU CANNO
YOU ARE A SYMBOL OF POVERT
THE BOTTOM FEEDER OF
CREATURES OF OPPORTUNITY,
AND LIKE THE RATS THAT
YOU WOULD MUCH RATHE
TO GET TO WHAT YOU
THAN WORK WITH EAC
TO BUILD TOWARDS WI
YOU ARE A LAZY,
MENTALLY INFERIOR
ALLOWING YOU TO
LETTING THE MONCE
MAR, JULLE IS EE
YOU RAPE YOUR OU
AND ABUSE YOUR O
NOW ALL THEY
MAY DO TO THE
JUST LOOK A
BEAUTIFULL
YOU HAVE P
AND NOW SHE

73

GRANDMA BLUES

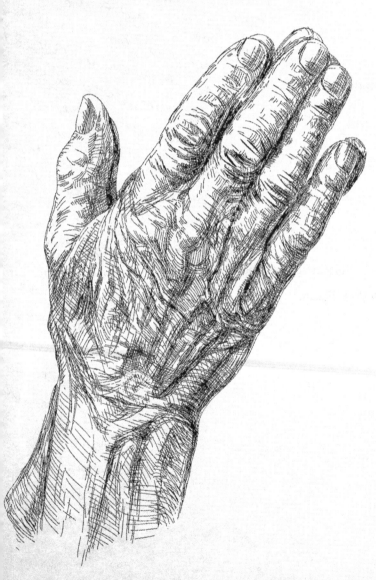

Grandma's in pain.

She often complains of how the aches of her ageing knees don't give her peace

And how she seldom dreams as she hardly sleeps these days.

But grandma says this one's beyond her,

She doesn't know what to do anymore;

Tried everything from throwing wooden spoons, to swinging electric cables.

Grandma has cursed at one point, even came close to throwing a knife to prove a point.

She's not afraid of going to jail, cause she says it's about time someone put Thembi in her place.

Grandma says Thembi is at it again, but this time grandma won't put up with the shame;

She is willing to strangle that little bitch back to whence she came.

Grandma is sick and tired of having to wait up late at night

Wondering whose father is driving her granddaughter home each night.

Thembi thinks just because she's had her first period and now has grown men groping themselves over her,

She is all that, now.

What baffles grandma's mind is how her granddaughter's thighs get to part at a bat of an eye.

Or even worse, how she seems to fall for an adulterer's lies.

As grandma sits with tears in her eyes and traces of sadness in her smile,

She continues to question whether these same men who failed at being fathers to their daughters,

Will grow up and realise that Thembi is twisted.

How sad they're not there to guide her

But mount her to prove their conquest.

It's these same men who should be guiding our daughters,

Not trying to guide their manhood into them.

Then they turn round and complain that youth have no respect these days.

How do they expect to be respected when they're out drinking and partying with youngsters?

And since when has it been a measure of a man's success to be seen parading and showcasing their latest teen conquests?

Grandma is in so much pain that even her forced laughter echoes in a valley of sadness as she continues to moan how Sizwe won't amount to anything more than his father.

He's already showing signs by fathering three first born sons and caring for none.

Sizwe truly is his father's son,

This is evident in the way he drinks and how he treats the mothers of his bastard daughters and sons.

Sizwe is a scumbag lower than low,

So much so that grandma hardly even mentions him.

How does one speak of a man who works two weeks straight, only to be paid with beers and straights?

Sizwe would disappear every payday Friday, only to reappear dragging home his spent carcass on Sunday.

Grandma bemoans the fact that she has never even eaten a sweet bought from Sizwe's pay

Yet she subsidises his trip to work every day.

Grandma is in pain again,

Though she often complains of how the aches that come with pain hardly seem to cease.

Grandma's biggest blues is sung from the fact that she has to watch her family disappearing generation by generation.

She has to watch this nation, disappearing generation by generation.

Grandma is in pain again, but this one ayinga ngaye.

WE HAD A PLAN

We had a plan; you and i.

We were going to revolutionize love.

We were going to stand outside the borders and laugh at those who were being held prisoners of love.

We were not going to toe the line for love, no!

We were going to be rebels.

We were going to love in our own way and it didn't matter who said what,

Cause we had a plan.

So it's not your fault that my heart faltered and found itself tripping and falling for you.

The heart wants what the heart wants,

This is how the taste of your name got to be tattooed upon my tongue,

And my breath found itself suffocating without your life-giving touch.

But it's truly not your fault cause we had a plan.

We were going to evolutionise love.

We were going to help liberate it from its leash of reason,

Free it from its prison,

Allow it to run as it was meant to,

Without limitation.

So, it's truly not your fault that my heart faltered and found itself tripping and falling for you.

The heart wants what the heart wants.

Now I have to sit here while the taste of your name is slowly removed from my tongue's memories,

And my breath has to learn to breathe again without your life-giving touch.

Yes, it's truly not your fault,

Cause we had a plan.

A REFUGE TO PIMPS, DRUG-LORDS AND NET DIE HERE
WEET WAT.
SHE HAS BECOME A WASTE-LAND,
EVEN DIE KAK OP SY STRAAT BEAR WITNESS TO THAT.
THEN YOU WUNDER WHY WE DIDNT WANT YOU TO PRO-CREATE.
YOUR OFF-SPRING,
THEY ARE MONSTERS LIKE THE SEEDS FROM
WHICH THEY FELL,
CONSTANTLY HIGH,
JUST TO TRY AND FORGET THAT,
THEIR FARTHERS WERE DRUNKERDS
AND MOTHERS WERE PROSTITUTES.
YOU SEE, YOU ARE ONLY A TOOL TO BE USED,
LIKE A SPADE,
USELESS WITHOUT YOUR MASTER'S GUIDING HAND.

DADDY'S DANCE.

He would stand to dance.

I would watch daddy stand to dance this dance

That was passed down from generation to generation,

From grandfather to father to son to grandson.

But this was no ordinary dance,

This was not like that bump jive that he and mommy would do,

Daddy bumping this way, Mommy jiving that way.

This was not even like the way he would tap his foot,

Snap his fingers; while whistling along to the latest jazz release.

This was a different type of dance.

This was a dance that only men danced before,

Even though it seemed that women were joining in of late.

I would watch daddy stand to dance this dance,

He would dance left; right, one; two.

He would dance arms waving, body shaking.

He would dance legs kicking, him ululating.

Daddy would dance, dance, and dance till he fell into this deep, disturbing trance.

That's the thing about daddy's dance; it always threw him into this deep, disturbing trance

Which would last and last and last,

So even when he got home at night, he would still want to dance,

And dance and dance.

He would want to dance with mommy as his stage.

Seeing that I could no longer watch daddy stand to dance,

I had to listen to daddy stand and dance.

Daddy would dance, left; right, one; two.

He would dance arms waving, body shaking.

He would dance legs kicking, shouting,

Daddy would dance all over mommy.

And mommy would bear daddy's moves

As though they were badges of honour upon her shoulders,

Without a whimper or a whine.

She would bear daddy's moves

As though any sound she would make would mean the death of her inner child.

Mommy would bear daddy's moves as though she was trying to protect my innocence.

I would watch daddy stand to dance this dance that was passed down from generation to generation,

From grandfather to father to son to grandson.

I would watch daddy stand to dance this manly dance,

All along hoping, no, praying, that I had not inherited this manly dance.

AZAMA

What is your country's name?

What is your country's name?

Do not give me the geographic positioning,

Tell me what the name of this country is and I will show you where freedom lives.

Like the Israelites, we still walk in the wilderness,

But I guess Moses could not stand this long walk to freedom,

Now he is long gone; we assume he's dead,

This is why we celebrate as though we've reached the Promised Land.

Yes, we're still camping by the road side and calling it home,

Hoping to keep living with our grant of free Quail and Manna from above.

What is your country's name?

We spit on our heroes names and dance on their graves as we celebrate our claim to fame.

They are the ones who fought yet we pretend they never stood by us.

They climbed the mountain to fetch the tablets with the law for us,

Yet as we climb the corporate mountain,

We simply shift, delete them from our memories.

Their names have been buried with their principles,

Their truths labelled as dirty politics.

What is your country's name?

Since we do not know where we are, how can we know who we are?

We need to forget what we've learned and retrace our steps –

Not back to our dates of births,

But back to the beginning of our humanness,

The beginning of uhuru.

What is your country's name?

Until you can answer this without feeling shame,

Then and only then can you claim true liberation.

Azania, I calling.

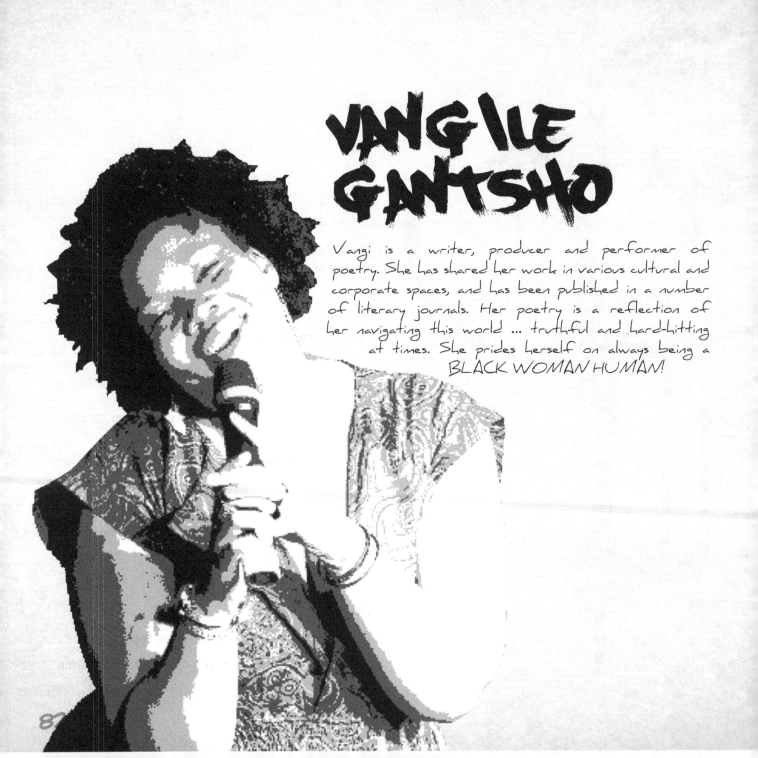

VANGILE GANTSHO

Vangi is a writer, producer and performer of poetry. She has shared her work in various cultural and corporate spaces, and has been published in a number of literary journals. Her poetry is a reflection of her navigating this world ... truthful and hard-hitting at times. She prides herself on always being a BLACK WOMAN HUMAN!

If Madiba were a hot air balloon

If Madiba were a hot air balloon
All that air would be guilt. And
It would be white. And
It would be the biggest balloon you've ever
                                        seen

Floating far above the sky
Up beyond the stars. And
We would all get to ride in it
All of us
Everyone
Except those whose tears it takes
to keep the air from coming out

                    Vaughn

LOVE WITHOUT CAUTION

I love you in ways my sorrow
cannot forgive
from a deep pit within my chest.

I carved you a throne
crowned you king and
fell victim to the tyranny
of your absence.

I love you in ways my sleepless nights
cannot overlook
beyond glistening eyelids
and imaginations that
spark hope.
I have painted you, my portrait
framed you, my masterpiece
neglected in the basements
of your absence.

You gather dust awaiting my death
your betrayal will emerge when I have passed
a vagabond will remove my dust
and relish in the fortunes of your smile,
never knowing the artist
behind the frame.

I should have burnt you at the stake
thrown your charms into the furnace
before your heat kissed my skin,
your flames devoured my cave.
I should never have let you
paint my breasts
with possibilities.

I should have forbidden you from filling my head
with thick grey lies.

But we love without caution.
And when that love is not
returned
we hurt without solace.

AT HOME, TONIGHT

I think my mother's gonna cry, tonight.

Her heart's gonna break

her soul will die, tonight.

You see

if my mother lays down on her empty bed, tonight

she's not gonna wake tomorrow.

I think my father's gonna kill my mother, tonight.

His cheating ways are gonna be the end of her

his infidelity, her last breath, tonight.

You see

if my father doesn't come home to her, to us, tonight

my father's gonna find her corpse tomorrow.

I think my brother's gonna have to be the man of the house, tonight.

His sister's gonna need him

his father's gonna curse him, tonight.

You see

if my brother plays that man, tonight

my brother's respect for his father's gonna be gone tomorrow.

I think I'm gonna kill my father, tonight.

My words, my actions will banish him,

and my father will dissolve into oblivion, tonight.

You see

if I know he's gonna kill my mother, tonight

my spirit just won't let him make it to tomorrow.

I think someone needs to end this madness, tonight.

Make him stop

and patch up this broken family, tonight.

IN HIS BLUE AND WHITE DOTS

I was 18 years young

First year, bright-eyed, bushy-tailed

We met at the hospital

We were both visiting him

She knew me

She called me a skanky ho

I called her a washed up hag

He assured me she meant nothing

She was 28 years old
Spinster, unmarried, childless

He was 30 years smooth
Successful, future bright, soon-to-be my baby-daddy

Seeing him in blue and white dots
Dots too big for a dressy shirt
Too drowning for his sunken cheeks
He wanted me to hold his hand
I wished she and I could talk a little

She was buried four months later

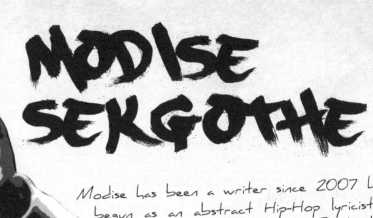

MODISE SEKGOTHE

Modise has been a writer since 2007 having begun as an abstract Hip-Hop lyricist. His exploration of Performance Poetry began in 2010 as a member of the UJ Poetry Society (formally known as the "Fore. Word Society"). He has headlined and performed in all their major annual shows as an individual and in collaboration with a number of other prolific poets. Aside from this, he has graced many stages throughout Johannesburg either in the form of slams, poetry competitions or open mike sessions and has quite recently explored other avenues of drama having thus far been part of four professional theatre productions under the UJ Drama Company. The first of these was "SA Shorts" which premiered at the Grahamstown National Arts Festival in 2012 and was also staged at the University of Johannesburg Theatre. This was followed by "The Boy Who Fell From The Roof" which was part of the "That So Gay Festival" hosted by the UJ Drama Company in 2012. In 2013, he participated in 'Equus' by Peter Shaffer, also under the UJ Drama Company.

CUNMLINGUS

With the whole world between her thighs,

I thrive to enter her centre.

First with my tongue… and then later, with my sceptre.

So I begin to transfer a message,

From her toes to her temple.

Spreading open her legs,

To expose and disassemble her rose,

With my tongue twisting,

Like that… of an elemental

I composed a sacred mantra,

And made her pose to begin our Tantra.

I'm supposed to be a little gentle

But still in touch with my inner-animal,

So I came close as though to attack her

But she proposed a better angle

From which her body was a triangle

And every corner was mine to handle… with care.

Before the engagement, I really need to prepare.

So my cunning tongue lingers at her base-

Chakra spinning out of control,

Anti-clockwise kundalini-spiral untangling,

The serpent strives when it's no longer dangling.

And her structure… begins to unfold, untangle, untold

Stories hidden between her groves

And the landscape of her thighs.

She moves to a silent rhythm,

Her breathe sounding a symphony astounding –

The epiphany of her drowning in my melody.

I conductor of the swirling serpent along her back,

My orchestra dances to a transient track.

And her cute bra… unravels the fruits of karma-sutra.

And through the diaphanous fabric covering her vase,

I can see the lotus positioned at her base,

Its petals seemingly spread all round her waist.

The incense of her aroma caresses me

As I nibble at her flower and dribble past her clit,

Gently licking her labia to penetrate the split.

Her scent I devour, her breasts like pendulous
dugs

Are the distance between our hugs.

Her back arched, her pelvis stuck to my mouth,

Yoga like positioning, my hands like Pilate
implements,

She is my instrument, she is my Himalaya

And even before I reach the top, she peaks.

The beat of her heart speaks to my art

As I reach for her most sensitive part;

Every touch a surprise, the slightest brush a
disguise,

Skins melting till one and another are no longer
distinct;

Instinct, the subtle dance of a universe in sync.

GUY DANCE (GUIDANCE)

Have you ever seen a guy dance?

Guided by the sky's hands,

Grenades explode with the slightest of his movements,

Followed by our eyes consulting each other

On what each and every move means.

An exuberance, a moving with complete sense,

Found in the image of his knees bent,

Pounding against his chest his heart is intent

On making itself known to onlookers

And move them to the greatest extent.

He's elated by the audience's collective scent,

Arching his body built to house his spirit in the shape of a tent.

From the bottom he rises as if levitating,

Gravitating towards heavens, a perfect ascent.

Heavens are sent in the guise of poems and dance

Where soldiers advance to peace through art.

Such rhythmic enchantments,

But stillness in all its beauty is also dance,

The movement of angels, Man in a godly stance,

Dedicated to the ebb and flow of a spirit in trance;

A ceremony of stars encountered by chance.

A sacred song plays as he kisses the ground with his feet stomping the sphere,

Flattening the earth to chisel a more levelled path away from the circle of fear.

His body chants, his bones bend but urge him not to break,

The voodoo of a vibrant soul thrashing and bashing against invisible walls,

Bursting free in dance, set to flee he dances patiently in the dark.

Have you ever seen a man cry?

His eyes leaking from having seen too many holes in his history.

Have you seen him tackle his misery?

Shackle his own feet and strangle himself for dreaming of liberty.

Have you ever been held hostage in your own bitter heart

In the name of a severed art

With tattered parts of yourself spread across the stage

As it continues to tear you apart?

Bit by bit, as parts of him are broken away, he lays stagnant,

Pinned to the weight of his mounted sins,

Ripping away at his flesh to reveal his truest skin and bone too thin.

He's prone to spin into a cyclone within,

A torpedo of strings on which he spirals and clings,

For the fire in his soul is the mother of his wings.

He desires to be told that he's fathered by a king.

Back and forth, his past is forced into his present.

He's tossed from his visions of heaven into this planet.

He hates the ground, its dust, dirt, graves,

And how it conspires with gravity to keep us low and earth-bound.

He's trying to find a way of screaming without having to make a sound,

A way of standing without having to touch this desecrated ground.

He wonders how there could be a point to a planet

Moving in circles, spinning round its sun,

Hanging about for centuries with no purpose

Aside from tragedy and a few rare glimpses of false fun.

It's a spherical prison designed so that none of us can ever run.

Thus my last question to you:

Have you ever seen a man die?

In the desperate hope to escape his host cause his sex is a hoax,

He prefers to be held in the hands of a man

But society detests his urges as a defiance of god's plan.

An abomination, a twisted perversion that can simply be healed

Under a preacher's hand.

Have you ever seen a guy dance?

Guided by the sky's hands,

Grenades explode with the slightest of his movements.

Have you ever seen a man cry?

His eyes leaking from having seen too many holes in his history.

Have you seen him tackle his misery?

Shackle his own feet and strangle himself for dreaming of liberty.

Have you ever seen a man die?

TRAVELLERS

A traveller once said to me:

"Throw away your compass and map if you really wanna arrive

Crush your navigator and dismember your radar if you truly want to find

Follow the wind

See your northern star during the day for the darkness in your heart can bring out its shine

Don't be shy, ask the flowers for direction and follow the walking eagle whose wings hold up the sky

Listen to it when it speaks, never wish to fly

For you have already arrived and are alive

Attune your foot-steps with the tortoise

Move as if not to disturb the air around you

Do not disturb the nothingness

Be calm my child

Speak as though in silence and the night will listen

Sleep my dear angel

The day is too loud for people like us

Don't be afraid to be alone, we don't belong here anyway

We were brought to collect the tiny dust-particles that fell from shattered stars

So look carefully but don't search

Let them find you

We don't have enough time; eternity is too near to people like us

We have stretched too far beyond our time

The truth haunts us

So stop yourself from living

Stay still and fulfill love's will

Don't work to improve yourself

Your already perfect forms lurks underneath your sleepy eyes during dim-lit skies

You don't need to prove yourself

Your presence evokes a heavenly essence in all those who see you…

Settled and content in seating in emotions of stillness

My dear child, your were brought here to swim

The ocean of earthly consciousness loves and embraces you, smiling with every wave

Be open, keep looking but don't search

The universe will speak to you but don't listen

The way will be shown to you but don't use your vision

Instead meditate

Keep your eyes closed and legs locked until you levitate

Let the world forget you ever existed

Kill yourself as soon as the sun sets but don't rise

Let the night last forever

But before that

Tell your loved ones never to cry and to save as much water as they can for the coming drought

For without or kind on this planet, it ceases to rain

The oceans follow us back to our home for their purpose here has been fulfilled

Empty the rivers in your pockets onto their palms

Tell them to keep their hands open and quench their thirst only when they see the sun again

There's no need for them to mourn

For you will not have left but will be logged right at the base of their fragile hearts

Tell your mother you love her

And that she was the heavenly gate that led you into this village called earth

Give her a peace of your soul

And tell her never to give birth for her gates were bolted with your arrival

The last divine seeker had been produced

And then it was done, the cycle had been completed

Finally the top of our spinning planet will come to a stop

All this will be not

Humans will be washed off the face of it like snot

There will be no trace of them but their scent

Which will linger until time's tale is cut off and its head crushed to a pulp

But that's all that will be left

Not their voices, not their actions but their scent

There never was a need to move, the never was a need to speak

Only angels in inner mountains waiting for you to reach the peak

All was planted within you

That's why you'll never find what you currently seek

Do not plant outside yourself

The fertile ground within you is the only place where you can reap

So go back home

Take your lover with you

There's a reason you recognised her

She was the weaver of your dreams but now that you no longer dream

You can awake to her beautiful face every morning

Tell no one of your departure

Let them feel it with the coming winds and remember the mystery in your shy eyes

Let them wonder at your demise as they did of your life and then let loose into the ether of the sun's youth

My dear child

Follow the coordinates of your djembe heart

Remember to ask the flowers for directions and follow the walking eagle whose wings hold up the sky."

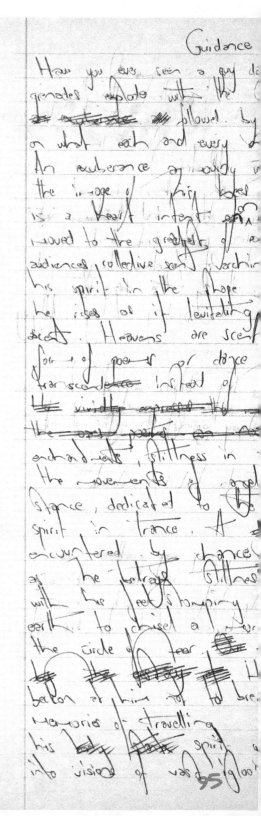

NTHABISENG JAHROSE JAFTA

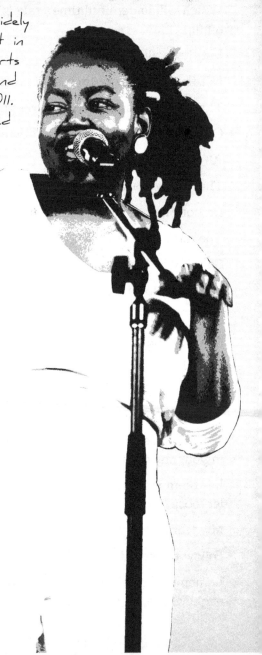

JahRose is a Bloemfontein based performance poet widely recognized for her contributions as both a writer and poet in the Free State since 2004. She has been involved in the Arts community as a poet, traveler, event Coordinator, mentor and author. Her company JahRose Productions was founded in 2011. She published and launched her debut poetry compilation titled "Rooted from the Heart", More recently she published the 'Free State of Mind' anthology which was coupled with an audio book as well as the launch DVD. This was followed by the 'Free State of Mind' film produced by Littlepond Productions available on YouTube. Coordinator of Macufe Poetry and Published Macufe PeoPress featuring various poets with PeoPress artists interviews available on YouTube, She also produced and published Harmony poetry and prose written by Harmony high school learners 2014, followed by the Peo series; PeoPlanters and PeoTree- Poetry is Fine Art project with Liako Ntsoele a fine artist from Lesotho and just published Mantlwane series which is children's literature

At present she is working on her much anticipated album which will be recorded with a live band.

BREASTFEEDING TOTAL SEXINESS

With his lips
He makes love
To my nipple
Sucks me
Milks me
Dry.

After the erect nipple
Soothes
His thirst
His hunger
He dozes off.

Oh, as he sucks, breathing sounds loud
In motion of give
Take
In
Out
The nipple my output
His tiny mouth the input
Warm vibrations!
Total sexiness.

PULA PAKENG TSA MAOTO

Hothwe ngwedi ha e kgelletse metsi
Ka mora matsatsi a supileng
E tla tjeka e shebe fatshe;
Nkgo e thubehe ho tsholla pula,

Pula pakeng tsa maoto
Se tlisa mahlohonolo
Se tlisa mpho
Ngwana badimo
Ho lebohwe Modimo
Ya ka hodimo dimo ho mahodimo.

bonqwanana bo emelle ka thoko
Bosadi bo hlahelle ka mahetla,
Ka ha tlhaho e o kgethile
E o ratile, ke mang a ka hlanohelang?

E hoba wena ha o feta
Le dinonyana di o binela
Pina ya kgothatso, pina ya lethabo,

Makala a difate a o fokela moya
jwalo ka kgosana, Mmapopelo wena Mmabophelo
Moemedi, motshehetsi, mohlokomedi
Tlouhadi, tauhadi , kwenahadi.

Ke a o lebohisa etong la hao
La bophelo
Maimemeng, mahlokong
O sa eme, o tshwarelletse
mme thabo, kgotso, kganya
O sa di bitsa le kajeno
tumelo, thapelo, tshepo
Di sale lemeng la hao ka mehla
Ke ka hoo, meloko e o latelang
E tla hlonolofatswa.

Moemedi. motshehetsi, mohlokomedi
Tlouhadi, tauhadi, kwenahadi.

Rain between the feet

As declared, the moon highly impregnated
After seven days as it twists and faces down
To shower in the rebirth
The calabash breaks to release torrents of rain

Rain between feet
Source of good luck
Usherer of Gifts
Chosen child
Of the ancestors
Praises to God
The Almighty

Girlhood asunder
Womanhood take charge
For nature has chosen you,
Adored you, who can argue against its destiny

For when you stride, sauntering
Even birds chant for you;
Melodious notes of courage, of joy

Leaves shelter you from the blazing sun
Blowing cool breezes for you
Like the princess,
Womb of mankind, you the source of Life
protector, supporter, care-giver
You, venerated elephant, lion, alligator

I congratulate you on your journey of Life
In turmoil, in melancholy
You stood the test of time, withstood storms.
Joy, peace and eternal light
You still beckon even to this day
Faith, prayer, trust
Still nesting on your tongue
Hence generations to follow your footprints
Their destiny shall be blessed.

protector, supporter, care-giver
You, venerated elephant, lion, alligator
Battle it up the women way...

*Translation: Tshidiso Masoloane

WOMB MEN

THE Comfortability that I feel
THE WARMTH around THIS DARK place Im In
Knowing of Cause THAT Light which is
hope & beauty Originates from #this Dark place

I'd expect even better
WHEN ~~actually~~ getting out there. &
THE FIRST TIME
I MEAN from all the HOUE I got
from my Round HOME
THE Sood THAT I RECEIVED
from food & Fluids
from TORNS 2 BONDS
THE Excitment & Joy I Felt &
Brought 2 the world AND PEOPLE

Close me.
WHEN EVERYBody around me WEHCOME ME
WITH SMILES & TEARS OF THANKSFULNESS
& Gratefulness.

I'd Sure Imagine it Being
THEE PARADISE. A place WERE possibilities
positivity & WISDOM RULES
~~~~ with TRUE LOVE

TATTOOED LINES

Somebody unseen
Decided
To
Tattoo
My
Skin

In no particular
Sketch or design
In mind
He did it!

Surpassed body butters
Oils and creams
Tattooed lines
Mapped none the less
Directed
Navigated
To teach me,
Show me
That
Life line had been extended
That

Blood line hasn't ceased flowing

These lines are drawn like
Alphabet carved
Read out loud
With foreign sound
Heard in the air
Like a song
With story told lyrics
A world grew here
An ancient soul rebirth
Life creations molded
Left the evidence
These lines will live
To tell a tale
That it was the unseen one
Who tattooed this skin map
Directions
Comprehensive
To mums
Stretched prints
Not even tissue oil can erase
They are as permanent as his fingerprints

KURT SCHRÖDER

Kurt Ludwig Schröder is poet/ storyteller based in Pretoria, South Africa. His poetry is based on personal life-stories and experiences, and he strives to create art that will "re-sensitize" a numb and desensitized world. He dreams of traveling the world, sharing his poetry as he goes.

SECRETS

There is a very particular excitement that
accompanies a secret.

It's the sweaty-palms, butterflies-in-your-stomach
thrill

of having special access to private mystery.
Tingling sensation,
secrets are wizardry.

The gentle bliss of mental deviousness,

thrill shifts to shame,
ignorance to blame.

Secrets are hooks in the dark
and now you're swaying,
suspended.

The thrill has ended.

Yes, secrets are wonderful –
until you become one.

REDEMPTION FOR RAPISTS
(THIS POEM IS A QUESTION, NOT AN ANSWER)

He shut out the judge as he passed sentence,

and instead concentrated on the four scars on his forearms

where tiny fingers had clawed for mercy,

as if it lay mingled somewhere between melanin and muscle.

He rides a flashback to the tussle,

remembering how he plundered the apple of his brother's eye.

Her name was Tsolofelo, an 11 year old African black pearl,

and he was the swine she was thrown before.

While the officers raised him from his bench,

he wondered if her young mother ever taught her that her name meant 'HOPE'.

Rising to stand, he was still staring at his feet.

How stark the contrast between his blackened overalls and her blue daisy pyjamas!

How tiny her pink and purple polka dot pumps had looked next to his

Big.

Black.

Boots.

Shuffling towards the exit doors,

he only lifted chin off chest to meet the burning gaze of his victim's mother.

Hell was in her eyes, and her tears could not douse the flames.

Yet, he savoured the moment their eyes locked,

because they seemed to unlock a war chest hidden deep inside of him.

He smiled,

as a single tear ran across the wasteland of his cheeks and clung to his jawline.

Despite her rage and despite his numbness, they both felt the increasing tide of relief,

however brief, and for whatever reason,

it was like the slow change of winter into new and

warmer seasons . . .

As he was led down the passage to his cell,

his fists were clenched – out of habit now, not hate.

He contemplated the emotional significance of hand gestures,

and maybe if his arms were arteries,

then his balled up fists were an aneurism,

stopping the anguish from bleeding out.

So he uncurled his fingers,

and pushed his palms upwards.

It reminded him of the way his grandmother prayed.

There were already nine men in the six man cell

but he was not bothered.

He had already, long ago, learnt how to be completely alone.

As a child, he had mastered solitude,

so he would never again be another's slave . . .

Chin up, chest out – be brave!

But now he's no longer sure bravery is a valuable trait.

And perhaps now it was too late, to say,

"Mama, won't you help me?

Mama, this is not my fault.

Mama, I need you now,

but I'm all alone . . . all alone."

But there was no one there for him.

The most concrete part of his world, now,

is the concrete floor against which his spine uncurls.

And he lies there, waiting for the past to attack, again.

He rides another flashback.

He is six years old, sitting on the edge of his uncle's bed.

He can hear the taxi driving away,

And he still wonders where Mama went that day.

Then there's the blur.

Warm smile, sweet talk, illusion,

Locked door, belt loosed, confusion,

belt strikes cheek, contusion.

Beat down, body weak, it's gruesome.

Arms gripped, body ripped, intrusion.

Can't shout, no breath, effusion.

Grinding teeth to pain, delusion.

Unconscious, bleed out, conclusion.

By the time it was all over,

the only soul he had left was the undersides of his

small,

brown

feet . . .

And, oh, how tiny they looked next to his uncle's

Big. Black. Boots.

He still wonders where Mama went that day . . .

The fury in that young mother's eyes is like disinfectant and Band-Aids.

A picture of what could have,

should have, and maybe would have been

if his own mother had burst through that locked bedroom door to save him.

He still wonders where Mama went that day . . .

But now, there is no more wandering in circles through the desert,

as the rivers well up in his exhausted tear ducts,

burst over banks and roar down his sullen cheeks

like healing waters flowing over dry lands.

For years now, he has fought to keep himself together.

He's a makeshift hand grenade

and that mother's eyes released the pressure pin . . .

freeing all his failing fragments to explode into sweet shrapnel.

He pulls up the left leg of his new orange overalls, and begins to untie the chord wrapped round his ankle.

The only tangible sign of his turmoil is two shoelaces tied into one.

Each from one of those

Big.

Black.

Boots.

As the shoelace noose tightens round his neck,

he is able to feel, but fights the panic and pain.

He is six years old,

waiting for his mother to burst through the cell doors,

and save him.

Is there redemption for the rapist?

"Henry"

I hate walking this way to class, because I know he's going to be standing around that next corner.
I can already picture the dejection set in his countenance. The contorted scowl of a man who has sunk his rotting teeth into every lemon life had handed him, and never learnt from the bitterness.

I bury my icy-hands a little deeper into my tracksuit pockets; partly to preserve my freezing fingertips from the frost-biting cold; partly to guide my thawing digits to the buttons on the side of my iPhone

I crank the loud up a few more bars; just enough to drown out the still small voice, nagging, and let stroll on in mindless concilliation. I ignore the feint ringing that begins pain-jingling in my eardrums.

I turn the corner

He is here today, again. Just like every other day before this tomorrows yesterday. I see him bowing down into his garbage bin altar, humming a song. A hymn perhaps. I was only grateful that his back was turned, and I quickly increased my cadence. I kept my eyes glued to the ground as I squirmed, snuck, slithered past him, hoping not to distract his attention from the one-man's trash, another man's treasure he was pillaging

Vuyelwa is a Joburg bred twenty-four year old who describes herself as a storyteller. "It is when I am most honest. It is also the hardest thing for me to hand my work over so publicly but I love being on stage, for me that sharing between an audience and a performer has the immediacy of church and communion. There is so much magic." Vuyelwa also has this to say about her poetry: "I owe my poetry to the township I spent my high school angst commuting from. Seeing the contrast between privilege and poverty just streets away from each other gives you perspective which can generate stories. It also gives you lots of characters to work with."

VUYELWA MALULEKE

BIG SCHOOL

On the first day of big school

when the teacher lowers her glasses

the old couple held together by

a weary frame, the unsympathetic ally

to her face before it started leaning

her shaky hands rocking the glasses along her crooked nose

to sit their heels into the trench of skin dug for the times

she needed to stand her eyes taller over them

so she could squint a scowl

at the naughty boy with a hot dog on his shirt

when her misty glasses are lowered for a scowl at you

as she says 'what's your name?'

her voice passes through the folds of cake and tea in her neck to you

you've practiced saying your name on a playground with friends

know the mermaid's skin it was sown from

could pick out the sound of each vowel

dropping on top of a zinc roof in a rainstorm

your name can play a game of hide and seek

and you who know it as well as your mother

will hear it giggle under the sofa

spy the small body hold its breath between

the mist of leaves in your neighbour's backyard

and since you don't know how to hate your name

don't know how to want it to be easy, a stripper's nickname

like stacy or jess or vee

you answer proudly langa/tsolofelo/nosipho/nozimanga/
mooketsi/ tsakani/andisiwe/lerato/
vuyelwa/thloki/boitumelo/kensani/

answer through custard cheeks with your parents
promise to you

when they ask for something easier

remember that promises worth making should
dry your mouth

and that you are a language without acronyms

to the child sitting in the middle of a classroom
with tables that swallow you

when she asks 'don't you have a Christian name?

you will learn later that there are 6,800 languages in the world

and each of them knows how to pray

so when she twists her eyes at your name

looks at the name list for something her tongue can lift

and reluctantly chokes. you. out. in. syllables

like a smelly meal eaten on a sweltering
summer day

in front of a garden boy she named Alex

this will be your first injury in big school

but all your mother will remember of this day

are your brave fingers and how they eventually
found friends and let go

your polished feet, the shiny pinch that made
you beam

she couldn't tell if your smile was nervous or in
pain

but she will remember it as a beginning

for you it will not be the last time

you repeat your name to call it off a ledge

built by a language that only lets you rent it

for public appearances and university applications

and poems like this, but it will never be yours

so for my children I will say

in the language of their name

every lump in your name

is my demand on the world for you

let those who can't fulfil each letter choke on it

for as long as your name holds a piece

of your parent's tribes in it, it'll be too big for some
mouths

still make them say it!

because only the people who can say it can see you

and baby, your soul is a face worth seeing

BLACK GIRL POEM

Black girl loan me your lonely
      don't bother washing it or giving it a
pretty press

let me have it at its worst and

I will keep it for you till there are more hands to
share it with

to show you joy you don't have to lie under, or
break your soul on to keep

so hand that lonely over

I will keep it in a book

it doesn't make you sexy or mysterious

honey you look sad

and don't tell me you ain't got none

our mothers have plenty lonely left over to share

under the bed, in a photo, locked to a date

lonely is the word you couldn't pronounce when it was your turn to read in a class of forty enemies

lonely is the friend who never called when your mother died

lonely is a father who didn't cry at your mother's funeral

told to stand on the whimper, raise his chest

and die a little

be a little man and big boys don't cry

and though he loves you

this old dog can never publicly hand over his

not even to soothe yours

and if it aint that deep let's write a book anyway

we'll call it survival in a white assed world

the pun will be intended

and you'll never go on another diet again

you will not shrink, or sink anything further

because you are gravity, perfect sense and karma

and it's your turn to shine

you hold the orbit of nations around those hips

like the gods had intended

and no one else can carry it like you

they'll call your strength, natural and amazing

they'll call you brave because that's what you are

but you've never believed in anything until a man said it was true

now take your lonely between your hands

find an ocean, learn to swim, find the ground of that ocean

and dig a hole and bury it

we've got to stop passing our damaged clutter down

it never looks good on anyone

'I don't care how pretty your face is,

no one can wear insecure and still get compliments'

this will the first line of a book

dedicated to black girls

and God ... I hope they read it

BLACK BOYS

Mothers, raven bearers of starless boys

thrown from that little bit of sky no one else
wanted

a Joburg corner everyone had farmed all the luck
from

you asked for no more than a chance of blunt
shine,

a grain your sons could make their dreams from

the knock on the door knew before you

when he didn't call to say he'd be late

that you would find his blood on the knuckles of
a street

along the unwatched curb **of** a grown man's fear,

in a gutter of a history he still walked through.

How could my baby be the boogie man

when his beard had just sprouted?

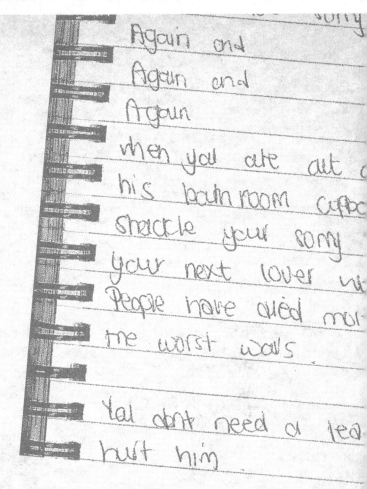

The boy with his skin shaded in, is suspicious

if he is a light brown he is the sick old joke
among slave owners and their maids

he is the boy they will hurry their steps from,

put their purses under their coats from

If your son looks like you, hide him

if your son has your cinnamon in him

he will be a sturdy brown casket

with skin as worrisome as his grandfather

and he had better glow in the dark

after six o'clock in winter

when the street lights are on

or you will find him dead.

And a white man with a gun will tell you he was scared

of a little brown boy with hands and screams for protection

and his mother nowhere near him.

Mothers of snuff coloured boys, borrowed boys

when this world has killed your son,

laid your best accomplishment in the dirt,

you will be alive.

Countless bags of tea will be lost to lipstick rimmed mugs that lifted past the dentures and the praying

of well meaning friends.

Thank them for drinking your tea with you.

Be grateful for your teeth but you are too old to make another son,

the leftover wreckage of your bellies

still remembers the boy you mourn –

how you rocked this Hail Mary to sleep

how your elbow held this small grace.

The empty rooms with their beds always made

will laugh at how silly you were to think

you could save him from this nervous world

with the baptized sound of your daddy's name.

Did you think grown men with guns could smell God

and the people who belonged to him second?

MY MOTHER SAYS

You don't need a gun to hurt him

pull your sins out against the sighs of another man's collar

but never let it touch his lips

it's ugly and rescuing like white Jesus on black skin

at home do it cleanly with the one you love

the one you would sing to

when you are a sober morning

when your voice is as beautiful as a broken violin

make it go further than the roof of your mouth

further than your nails under his skin, than the dressing table, further than the door

and though you know how this one likes his eggs, where his books are in your room

how his chest sleeps on your lap, unguarded, watching something you like

he is not the only one you will bend your bones for

like sacrifice, like revenge, like salt

by means of a god who crumbles between your bodies

you are the breath at the end of a dog chase you started

do not be sorry, he will not keep you to practice forgiveness

do not be sorry, he will want again and again and again

after you are out of his mouth, his bathroom cupboard, his grocery list

shackle your sorry to your tongue and love your next lover with it

put your sorry back in your mouth,

people have died more desirable deaths in worse wars

you do not need a leaf-shaped-dagger to hurt him

girls like you are always attractively disfigured

with all your holes on the inside

no one to visit the wounds

it is hard to count what's missing

what's wounded and too harassed to heal

was it your first heartbreak that did it?

or was it your father's paper boy hat, swung sideways

laughing for women who were not your mother

and now your hands, holding someone else still feel like loss

you are the unattended wounds of a genocide on trust

you are blood where there should be milk,

you are not the words in his love letters

you are a postcard place he'd want to write from for a month

but he'll leave sick with the immigrants grief

unable to find an address to call home

not until you agreed about how to build your house,

what shade of grey to make the kitchen counter

how many rooms for the lies?

how many lovers for each bathroom?

and who would clean their hair out of your shower and your bed

full with your conversation?

and would all your children be his?

we are all refugees of loves that were good to us once

whose food we could trust to not make us sick and ugly, till they did

so no you do not need a gun or a leaf-shaped-dagger

you do not need a witch with her grandmother's spell

you do not even need her grandmother

to hurt him all he needs is to find a girl like you

and when you are hurting, despite the pain suggesting that you might

you will not die and that might be love

but that is love you cannot die next to

NoLIFE

NoLIFE (Nobody Lives ForEver), born Carlos Ncube, is a writer, rapper, performer and poet. He started writing at the age of nine after being inspired by his uncle "Snooty King" — from whom he got his first stage name 'Snooty Carl'. After years of being a battle rapper, in 2011 he discovered Word n Sound, and was, from then on, inspired to write poetry. His writing style is a mixture of the metaphysical school of thought and conscious rap, both brought to life by his powerful delivery.

ANGELS CAN ONLY CARRY ANGELS
(TO KEAMO)

Yes, babies fall from the sky, shed their wings and fall into the wombs of the desired counterpart

Diligently moulded into a part and set never to part because the path selected rejected the legs of many...

But yours labour in a complete cyclic enigma of purity that settled innocence in the belly

It's godly intelligence that when a foetus kicks it is confirmation that you will forever walk together! COMMunication in UNITY

Melted into a community of two hearts for the journey of life begins with you, Mother

You, the beacon in darkness for when days are bleak your shoulders light up the destiny of recovery

When my knees seem weak and I cannot speak, I seek. And find your voice folded into my heart as we are one till death does us apart and my umbilical cord is the ring, through which we confirmed our union

Angels can only carry angels passing stars right down to the rediscovery of a "milky way"

Scientist say there are more stars than grains of sand so I think you were made of star dust in abundance

That's why the melody of your pulsations is "twinkle twinkle little star, precious baby I know who you are"

So long my home.

So long my home, So long my home
So long my home, I'm coming
So long my home,

I am too young to understand, perception and
hind sight is a common struggle for a born free,
But not so far from Reality I hear tales of
how we have come to be.

Shackles Broken where land was a prison for those
who Roamed Before the arrival of ABE(ungu. Spirits
of the gods is what they were thought to be.

And a submissive nature diluted by an epiphany, what
was siphned over was rebelled for, to civilize a nation
is to please god by forcing land is blasphemy

Where did we go wrong our only sin was skin if
-you overlook their point view, psychologically fit to
earn peanuts and own little. sea? segregation wedges
a society apart

Slave Labour of a meagre kind elders with broken, because
Where you grow is your pride, all you have in need
to survive, But a measly 7% is what was left
to stay alive

ABSURDITY FROM 1994

Perfection takes time

Arrested development that made me lose my mind

The mathematics of existence tryna find the day that im'a die

Cos I heard, that tears fall from the storm's eye

It's how they play on fears, when you forget yourself, they:

Bruise and they batter but what does it matter?

They always try to be didactic with the propaganda

But we all gotta get paid, so where is the common sense?

Masseuse for the brain cells when thoughts are always

I'm not taking any chances so you can and place your bets

The exodus of excellence/intelligence in resonance is written in the genesis

It's common biblical fantasy, for all the fellas that are tryna see, all the fallacies

They planting seeds, but who's gonna pay for your generations apathy

Sitting helplessly?

So they finalise lies, to cut ties and get by

Wanting a piece of that pie, but it stings 'cause B.E.E. was meant for that black guy who's watching rain fall from a black sky

And the taunting pain stays, look into his eyes and you will see

The thought stains

Heaven is only a breath away, but until that day.. things will never change

BLOOD DIAMONDS

Raw beauty can cost you an arm and a leg but you battle to save your wealth while we lose our limbs so you can gloat.

Your humanity has been tainted by greed. You have become commercial zombies, waiting for an apocalypse, starving yourselves to death, because the truth is hard to swallow.

You know nothing about happiness. Just look at how your children over-indulge in emotional blackmail. Personalised spiritual poverty and you've even been blacklisted by depression. Money can buy you misery when your soul is auctioned for a gun.

Diamonds are a girl's best friend … only if she knows they are encrusted with the hunger that could silence the insatiable behaviour of obese children, polished by the blood of men who no longer know compassion.

These hands were meant to build a future but there are cracks in the foundation of the present.

Feet have become callous, so I can no longer stand my ground. I used to move mountains for my wife and now … I am sifting stones, under the guard of a puppeteer, pulling invisible strings attached to an AK47, all for the cause of an affluent man to speak the words "I LOVE YOU" in vain? There's nothing noble in getting down on one knee, if your feet have never been stabbed by thorns in the bushes, while attempting to dodge bullets that scribble the fate of innocent people into heaven.

Engraved in a mass grave, the stench of rotting corpses, returning to the soil. And maybe, just maybe, they could also become gems because the human body is made of carbon which is part of the chemical make up of diamonds.

The reason a wife-to-be is smiling, is the same reason my people are dying. Humiliated by fear and my dignity lost somewhere between a soldier's foreskin and my rectum.

So, tell me, what do you know about fear? When my son is only 13 and he holds a semi-automatic machine which constitutes a firing squad and he points it at me, to free the African leviathan, disguised as a human, in an office, with Bipolar skin.

Neo-slaves and the agony in free labour, only to be paid in death by the Grim Reaper who wears a bandana, has one eye missing and his weapon of choice is a machete.

They lied when they said that there is a lack of jobs. All it takes is the death of one to even the odds. The Promised Land was bought for tobacco and now … De Beers is a God.

There is blood on the hands of Naomi Campbell …

Remove your hands from the war. Remove your hands from politics. That message was clarified when my wife was 9 months pregnant and they slit her stomach open, right before they used her umbilical cord as a noose and hung her off a tree.

When rationality seizes to exist, you fight to protect the emotional assets of your affection. But what's the point in fighting for a corpse, especially if you do not have any hands? The truth maybe subjective but we . . . are dying for the diamonds they wear.

And to cover up the brutality, they label them American-Swiss diamonds, which is absolutely ridiculous because Switzerland doesn't have any natural resources. And you call their bluff by heeding to the digits of death in a meaningless stone that breaks my bones.

We bleed for no value. So the question is, what price would you pay for these diamonds? What price would you pay?

I STAND CORRECTED

The law of nature dictates that procreation is purpose . . .
But the incipient insolence of your kind has flourished into intransigence,
blatant disrespect in the house of the Lord.
God made man on the 6th day and, as a matter of fact, to be exact,
created women in second place as a subordinate extract.

So tell me, do you think because society is patriarchal, being a woman dating
another woman is some sort of empowerment?
Typically used as props of freedom in the constitution just to lift a burden off
the government?

Bitch! You are dressed like a man but I can see your curves and I'm loving it.
And they say if it's broken it can be fixed.
Homosexuality is a psychological disorder and my penis is the mental institution,
the relevant remedy to your insanity.

Remember that estrogen is ruled and completed by testosterone.
So I am here to set you straight. I'm not a threat.
I just want to show you a good time while I'm inside you like bad breath.

Rights can only extend as far as you are willing to protect them. But you are looking pathetic and weak.
Right now I just want to teach you a lesson but I'm also attracted to the pheromones you reek.

Lady:

"But you're an idiot if you're going to measure my character using masculinity as a scale.
'Coz if that's the case, then the only women in here are the two of you.

Spicho:

Thulamaan, eymfethu. Ithing; khulumenaye lo muntu.
Woman, you should only speak only when you are spoken to.
For now let your labia do the talking.
Your ovaries are exhausted; your body was made to carry children
but you are forcing yourself to be a barren desert of abundance
with the fruits of a fallopian tube's labour left to rot.

You should have your skin pulled off your body for displacing
future generations in your affection for another woman.
This incessant talking of equal rights will have you smashed by a train –
and you should be afraid of the garrulous conductor.
You're going to be a woman by the end of the night.
Your tears are going to be evidence of your feminine nature.
I'll squeeze screams out of your masculine character
because you are in denial of the reality of your oocytes.
So, vaginal monologues will be silences by erectile soliloquies
You don't deserve the luxury of life
So please understand my frustration with your disability.
Sfebe, you should bend over once you get on your knees.

Sex with the corpse of a lesbian has always been my dream.

Darkee:

>Eh Spicho mfwethu, let's get out of here, she's
>well
>
>On her way to burning in hell.

Spicho:

>Hai maan, I'm about to come, what's the rush?
>
>Just run around the house and see if you can
>find a toilet brush.
>
>We'll put it inside her before we leave.
>
>This is theatric violence Mfana they won't
>believe

SILENCE...

My spirit hovered inside the room.

Two men flee the scene.

My body on the floor

With blood trails around it to show the places
that I have been.

But death followed me silently

So you can take this as an apparition's litany.

Father, it is not their ignorance.

Please forgive this society.

Sometimes feelings are insensitive to
expectations.

My mother always blamed Satan for my sexual
inconsistencies,

Dragged me to church,

But the only thing that a prayer could do ...

Was anger me

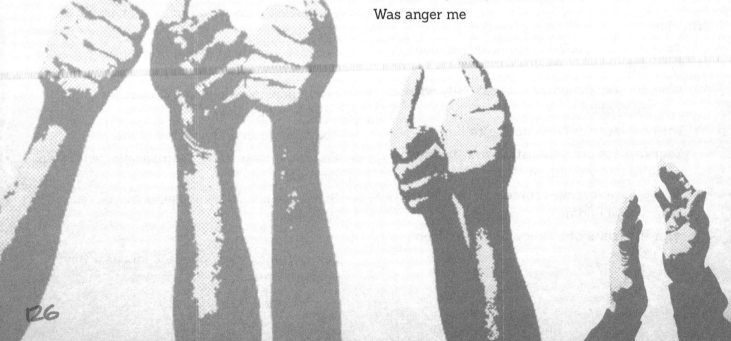

Misunderstood because Africa is exclusive to:
Men provide and women

In the kitchen.

Men provide and women in the fucken kitchen.

It's not like I couldn't perform these tasks.

But my disposition towards rejecting any man
who would woo me,

Was a disorientation towards God's injunction.

But my choice was a direct result of biblical free
will.

And so the apples of my eye were all of a
homogeneous make up.

They should have remembered having a Vagina
does not translate into

Attraction to the male species.

But this is Africa and having personal preference
is a disease.

`First I'm judged for my decisions. Being told
things like,

"You should be dating men 'cos you have a pretty
face."

Now these bastards have raped .. trying to set me
straight.

Secondly, I'm discriminated against because of
my race.

I don't even know why I have dreadlocks.

And I don't know if people know this

But Rastafarianism in its essence is homophobic.

But finding a 'cure' defies logic –

Pardon me, it's the same mentality that has
grown men

Raping babies trying to get rid of HIV.

I got judged for trying to choose my happy
ending

And instead my character gave me a life sentence

And now .. I Have NoLIFE.

So .. do I stand corrected?

127

CLINT SMITH

Educator and poet, Clint teaches English at Parkdale High School in Prince George's County, MD, USA. In the classroom, he combines his passion for poetry and justice to teach students the importance of their own stories as catalysts for meaningful social action. Outside of the classroom, he serves as the school's slam poetry coach and is the founder of Collective Voice for Justice, which empowers and trains students to become community organizers. In 2013, Clint was named the Christine D. Sarbanes Teacher of the Year by the Maryland Humanities Council. He has been featured in the Washington Post and is profiled in the book, "American Teacher: Heroes in the Classroom" (Welcome Books, 2013) as one of the top 50 educators in the US. In addition to teaching, Clint is an Individual World Poetry Slam finalist and was a member of Washington D.C.'s 2012 & 2013 National Slam Poetry Teams. In 2012, he served as a cultural ambassador to Swaziland on behalf of the U.S. State Department where he conducted poetry workshops on HIV/AIDS prevention, cross-cultural understanding, and youth empowerment.

LESSONS FROM A SENEGALESE VENDOR

In Africa,
    A land the history books tell
    is supposed to be my home,
    though here, I am made to feel more
    of an outsider than ever before.

I go to the stand of a man
    selling mangos on the corner.
    Searching the cotton pits of my pockets
    for coins that still contain
    the faces of their European colonizers.

I look at the vendor,
    his polished, charcoal skin. The way
    his hands glow against the orange fruit.
    A darkness that reminds me of bedtime
    stories read to me by my father.

I have seen him before,
    He is the griot. After evening prayers,
    he gathers the children round, teaching
    them lessons through stories passed down
    from the heavens. When he sees me,

He stares at me like a jackal,
    Vous etes une mettise qui viens
    d'Etas Unis, non? You are one of those
    mulattos who come from America, no?
    No, I say. I am black just like you.

Shaking his head
    You are not like us. He turns around to observe
    the shore behind us, as riverboats bobble
    between the shifting tides. He says, Our skin
    is like the jagged rocks that line this beach, and

You my son are the sand.
    Merely a collection of withered pieces
    that has eroded from our foundation.
    At one point we were the same,
    but we are no longer.

To escape,
    my apparent impurity,
    I pull a photograph
    of my parents
    from my wallet.

Holding my caramel thumb on the photo:
    between my father's olive skin as he lays
    his pursed lips upon my mother's light
    and luminous face, I create
    a spectrum of brown among us.

I place it in his hand.
    After examining the photo, he looks up at me,
    as if analyzing the coordinates
    of the freckles on my cheeks.
    None of you are like us.

WE ARE BLACK BOYS IN AMERICA

We are charred vessels,
vestiges of wood and wonder.
Anchors tethered to our bows.
It is the irony of a ship burning
at sea. Being surrounded by
the very thing that should have
saved us.

Anthology

The literary canon is
an artifact of exclusion.
It will render your words
flightless.
A kite slashed by wind
that could not carry it.
The spool remains in
your hands, though you
have never been given
the string by which to tie it.
Each flight a flurry of failures.
The earth you walk on,
soon draped in an autumn
of grounded constellations.
Our stars not meant for their sky.
We have never known the same
horizon.

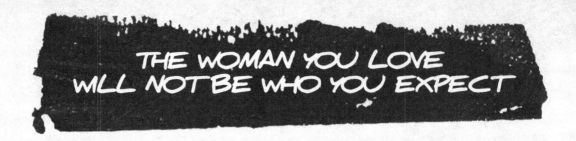

THE WOMAN YOU LOVE WILL NOT BE WHO YOU EXPECT

The brown in her skin

will come from a different place

than your own.

Your histories will have only

ever been whispers on the underside

of one another's tongues.

Her stories of white men who came to her country,

tried to bludgeon what was holy

and turn it in to another form of sacrament.

Your stories of white men who brought you to theirs –

how you run through this world

still shackled to their last name.

Her name will be a coalescence of syllables

your family cannot pronounce.

Remind her that it is only because our mouths

have never housed such magic in their midst.

You will proceed cautiously,

wary of how someone could

see the secrets in your eyes.

You will no longer be an enigma.

She will ask you,

"Why?"

"Why?"

"Why?"

She will ask you questions

you were always too scared to ask.

This will frighten you at first

as you realize mirrors

do not only reflect back the parts

you wish to see.

It is the first time you will see yourself for who you are.

But do not let this frustrate you.

She will give you so much

and it will take time to think in two
instead of one.
It will remind you that you are
not good at math.
Learn to go back and correct your answers.
Do not mistake erase marks for weakness.
It's okay to acknowledge
the things you didn't know.

When you tell her you love her
she will look at you intently.
Do not mistake the silence for doubt.
She is only trying to measure the memories in
your eyes.
Her past has taught her
that these words can make a mockery of time.
When she says it back,
do not be afraid to show her every part of you.
Walls of hay can be painted to resemble brick.
There are parts of you that will need rebuilding.

Give her a shovel and cement, she will be willing
to wear the hardhat if you let her.

You will meet her earlier than you thought
you were supposed to.
Treat your plans like that first draft that they
were.
You have to be okay with changing the plot
if it makes for a better ending.

Your best poems will come from your
conversations.
Remember that on the days you feel you must
choose one or the other.

Ash-Leigh Lex LaFoy is the brainchild of her predecessors formerly known as Lexikon and Queen Shalabeama, with 'LaFoy' being her real surname. Originally from Durban, now based in Johannesburg, having made her mark as a Freestyle, Battle and Performance MC and Poet over the past 9 years, Lex LaFoy evolved into who she is now: Lex LaFoy the Rap Pop star. She has performed and participated on platforms such as Poetry Africa, Shiz Niz (ETV), Red Bull's first Bass Camp 2013 and continues to excite crowds, making waves in and beyond South Africa.

LEX LAFOY

THE SUN

The Sun brings light.

The Sun shares light.

The Sun is light.

The Sun is chemically enabled to breathe light.

The Sun wakes up.

The Sun feels a need to actively radiate change,

The Sun does.

The Sun feels an affiliation to the stars.

The Sun is told by another Sun that the stars probably see stars when they look up at us.

The Sun laughs.

The Sun re-all-eyes-is the Egyptian god Ra/Re,

Personifies thee.

Aspect of self: embodying de-

Lightful existence.

Deities incarnate eternalistic descriptions.

Epical Hindi mistreated women turn Goddess.

We matter so much, we flesh!

Reawakening the power of affection

Our souls occupy an intangible caress.

The Sun rises. The Sun sets.

What next?

The Sun reads, learns, grows then flourishes.

The Sun reaffirms its place in the system. The Solar System.

The Sun re-members its ability to actively organize the orbits of those around it,

decoratively putting to function the 13th moon omitted by months count.

Why? Could that have been too much of a mouthful?

Or was that elitist knowledge out of bounds?

The Sun's secret societies are no longer secret.

Knock and the door shall be opened,

Seek and ye shall find.

We've encountered Knight Templar reads, Osiris'
Teachings,

Seth Speaks, African Woman, the Original
Guardian Angel, Thor and More.

Sun please.

I pray, when the Sun looks the Sun sees.

Discovered on the back of a toilet door in St.
Augustine's:

Our saline content,

Meaning our ratio of salt to water,

Is exactly that of the ocean.

Now what's this?

Commotion or co-incidence?

I flinch at the fat blatant fallacy of that word's
surprising tone.

What?! The hand of perfect timing, the knowledge
of the all knowing hadn't known?

That 'Sun', like 'womban', a grammatical era,

Was altered during the Middle-Ages,

After the likes of Chaucer brought literal fire to
the pager

Where no orthodox spelling was imbursed.

Get on the net; connect and I-burst

And search for a history that lives in your memory

Waiting to be reimbursed.

Sun, Heavenly Body, Celestial Being.

I still Party,

'Cos I heard dance is the highest form of worship.

And we honour the momentum given to us when
used

So free self from that state of inertia.

Hi, my name is Ash-Leigh, rooted Ashtree,

The sister of Tersha,

The grand-daughter of Faith

who is the Daughter Sun of the Sun

who married that Sun, who's the Sun of the Sun
of the Sun.

3 mins.

⊥ saviourtude of Motherhood
⊥ fresh perspek! purpose konek!
all-knowing, call collect
⊥ origin, ⊥ quintessential
⊥ proprietor ⊥ highest credential
THAT! MOTHER! is! YOU!
THAT! WOMBAN! is! YOU!
⊥ mountain in ⊥ distance
⊥ ordinator of every wishlist
⊥ warmth ovulator, ⊥ operator,
⊥ marvel-maker, ⊥ vision on
blank paper
THAT! MOTHER! is! YOU!
THAT! WOMBAN! is! YOU!
⊥ smile, ⊥ face, ⊥ countenance,
⊥ grace, ⊥ river, ⊥ fountain is
⊥ hologram
⊥ witch, ⊥ healing potion. AUGET!
⊥ source of sourcery! ⊥
of sacred geomet
thru binary fiboon
of giving

137

MOTHERHOOD

The Saviourtude of Motherhood.

The fresh perspec'! Purpose connect! The All-Knowing Call-Collect!

The Origin. The Quintessential.

The Proprietor. The highest credential.

That Mother - is You.

That Womban - is You!

The Mountain in the distance. The Ordinator of every wish list.

The Warm Ovulator, the Operator. The marvel-maker, the vision on blank paper.

That Mother - is You.

That Womban - is You!

The Smile the Face the Countenance.

The Grace the River the Fountain is . . .

The Witch. The healing potion. Auset!

The source of sorcery! The well of sacred geometry!

The Earth, through binary fission

Giving birth to the Moon.

The Risen belly. The Uplifter. The One who . . .

Concludes. Who soothes . . .

That Mother - is You.

That Womban - is You!

The Spice the Flavour. The Wise old womban. The Maiden. The Dress-maker.

The tailor.

The loop-in. the blessing the blissing.

The Favour.

The paint the material. The canvas the super-surreal!

The impressionist! The fair perspective yes! The affectionist! The air, the labour!

That Mother - is You.

That Womban - is You!

The tight jeans.

The RNA that coagulates our genes.

The bright attire! The very seed that inspires!

The attitude! The vicissitude! The "Miss-You-Too".

The unconditional love she radiates as a soulHer soul root flying high.

Her umbilical – a kite.

Connect her to the ground yet keep her heavenly sky.

That Mother - is You.

That Womban - is You!

Sarah -The wife of Abraham!

Yashoda who lovingly took Krsna in!

Maria and Mary Magdalene!

Dinah – the 13th tribe!

ISIS! Modjadji! The Enki!

The sky! The night!

Athena! Nomkubulwane! The Bride!

The princess! The Snow White!

Mother Theresa. Ma'at!

The keys played by Alicia!

The heart!

The fore-front!

The Rosa Parks!

The Empress Menen, Makeda, Makeba

Mangonyama!

SING!

For That Mother - is You.

That Womban - is You!

AMBITION

I am possessed...

By this idea

And I, dear, cannot find an alternate outlet.

For this 'found dead,

and unmarried' haunts me.

Like, 'why aren't you married yet?

mm? Rapper girl.

Raunchy?"

For the marriage of spirits is divine

yet,

so is connectivity

and so is time

And,

femininity is no fine a line we cross on the Greenwich.

Centered

Co-ordinated

Principal

Inaugurated

Chosen

Favoured

Highlighted

Laboured

To bring forth a force

according to The Calling and cause

in the form of:

unchanging laws and claws.

As for that self-empowerment ish we preached back in 2005, 6 and 8,

The New Age has dawned

and if you hadn't reached the feats of the noosphere... too late

they say.

For the breach of the divide is wide

and what was once catastrophically prophesied as Dooms Day

is in actuality (all superstition aside)

the polarity of thought

come alive.

I tried to correct their patterns

like Life cried at the feet of our actions.

Permeating soul into the detached

pumping blood into bricks and thatch.

Now The Builders build on

unperturbed by conspiracy and song

that was created to mask the face of a fate that
was written loooooong ago.

What we CAN alter is the personal

the individualized experience

while subscribing to a God concept as Merciful

I would like to tell you that church was full

this past Sunday.

However,

word got out that we are God

and people are now circling the roundabout

like planets to a Sun

round about the first time we conceptualized our
first memories

before we saw ourselves as enemies.

With borderlines and difference

remember the memories inherited across time
and distance?

Memories, past or present

projectories

into a hell or heaven.

This ambition they call the devil

that severs me

from the mould of genetic cycles and meddles

in the no-go zones –

like 'We do this like this

because we've been doing it like this

and will continue to do so until the ozone folds".

Yet, as with the invention of print

ideas, sporadic in the wind

have germinated into a phase of no return

and while they continue to experiment and fuck
up the quality of our education

we STILL learn.

In the ambiance of this ambition sits the
seedlings of potency

well-earned

sacrificed with the lives we fertilized and then
returned.

This ambition lives through me

FIGHTING, for my turn.

IainEWOKrobinson

32yr old iainEWOKrobinson is a Hip Hop flavored Spoken Word activist. He's a professional Aerosol Artist, actor, published poet and recording artist, part-time English teacher and a fulltime father. He operates internationally from Paris to Medellin but his head and hind quarters remain firmly planted in "Poison City" Durban, South Africa. Both of his anthologies are available through Echoing Green Press. He thinks he is being followed @ewokessay.

GARDEN BOY? KITCHEN GIRL?

Never called a man boy
Never called a woman girl
All I'm saying is I'm simply praying for a simple world

Never called no cat 'kaffir'
Never named another 'nigger'
See I always tried to amplify my vocab, keep it bigger
See I believe the smaller the vocab, the bigger the bigot
So I maintain and train a million ways to say 'Frigg it!'
    'Frigg it!' meaning 'FUgettaboutit', say it how you want to
    But depending on who hears you, don't say I never warned you
    The same way that some say that some words contain you
    Some words will form you, some words are used to frame you
LIKE   a man called boy
    A woman called girl
    (History got me saying I'm simply praying for a simple world)

See, simply put, boys don't work in gardens, men do,

> Coz sowing seeds, nurturing growth and
> harvesting fruit is far too critical a concern to
> leave it up to boys.

> So it's true: boys don't work in gardens, men do.

See, it's so simple, girls don't work in kitchens,
women do,

> Because feeding a family is sustaining a
> society and it's more than stirring a soup or
> peppering a pot (that's what girls do).

> That's why girls don't work in kitchens, women
> do. Simple. True.

SO   I never called a man boy

> I never called a woman girl

> I just stayed praying saying please for a

simple world.

(See I been warned, words are how I'm formed
Some words contain you, some used to frame you
So I'm working my words into frames for me to use
Hammering shields out of swords for use against abuse)

SO   when I'm saying "I'm praying", don't look
for God when I do

> When I'm saying "I'm praying", it's to myself,
> I pray to you

> I'm praying like meditations on my mind,

> Like it's simple, treat us all like we're all one
> of a kind

> of human being human, don't need a book
> to make that true man

> I'm praying that I'll be treated the way that
> I treat you man

> I'm praying for that humanity

> Praying for that sanity, for you to accept
> responsibility

> and not hand it to some deity

> Some Supreme Being, unseen, to leave you
> all free

> to be seemingly Sinners or Saints

SO   Deity? Whether there is or there ain't, I'm still praying

for that sanity

So when a two year old girl is raped by a grown man

I don't have to hear you tell me that "God has a plan."

And you won't have to hear me reduce my vocabulary, like the worst bigotry,

Like FUCK YOU man! If that's Gods plan then it's fucking bad

And it shouldn't be followed by any sane woman or man

Coz it's only boys and girls who paint fantasy scenes

While men and women break their backs to let their children dream

And I call that man boy and I call that woman girl

Who wants to sacrifice reality for the sake of a fake world

Who wants to swop the present for a story about heaven

The wrong words are all it takes to lessen any lesson

I'm saying I'm praying that we can keep the world simple

So a man called boy becomes a strategic symbol

The simple strategy is working words non-stop

Coz with words working, none stop the seed cycle to the crop

and the garden crop become the kitchen cook

a full stomach means the difference between a bigot and a book

Never called a man boy
Never called a woman girl
All I'm saying is I'm simply praying for a simple world

THE HEAD, THE HAT AND THE HEART

[thought one]

If the heart had to have a hat then the head would be that / the head would be the hat of

the heart / the heart's hat: the head would be that hat / and the head is much higher then

the heart so if the head were the heart's hat then the head would have to be a hi-hat…

Bring a BEAT if you wanna be where it's at

where the beat's at BE where the beat's at BE

where it's AT

be at the beat

BE at the beat where its AT

where it be

where it's at

where it BE AT

the BEAT

BE AT

the BEAT the BE AT the BEAT…

the heartbeat be where the head be at / if the heart be the head then the head be the hat /

the head be the hat of the heart with the heart/ beat the head with the heart/beat the heart

where it start / the head be the hat of the heart with the heartbeat BE AT the beat BE AT

the heart BE AT the head BE AT the start / beats in the head like a steady heart / beating

the head with a heavy heart / beaten the heart when the head is heavy / so UPBEAT the

heart to lift the head / steady

SO

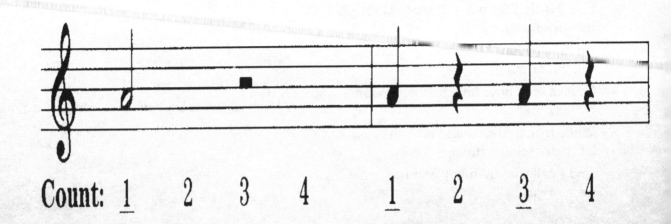

Count: <u>1</u> 2 3 4   <u>1</u> 2 <u>3</u> 4

146

Count: 1   2   3   4   1   2   3   4

[thought two]

the head be the hat where the heart be at / when I lift my head then I lift the hat / see you

so I signal you with acts like that / recognize my eyes and lift your hat back / the heartbeat

be where the head be at / if the heart be the head then the head be the hat / the head be

the hat of the heart with the heart/beat the head with the heart/beat the heart where it

start / the head be the hat of the heart with the heartbeat

SO

lifting the hat is raising the head is keep the heads up for days up ahead / coz "I see a bad

moon..." but that's not all that's "...rising." / if the

hat won't fit the head needs resizing / if the head won't lift the heart needs reviving / with a tip of the hat I can see we're surviving /

when the heart skip / then the hat flip / but we're in it together / that's the point of the tip

direct the tip towards you

point the tip towards you

in your direction the point I tip in / I point the tip in / I point tip in / point tip in / point / tip in /

point / tip in

point the tip towards you

direct the tip towards you

when the heart skip / then the hat flip / but we're in it together / that's the point of the tip

1 and 2 3 and 4 1 and 2 and 3 and 4 and

[thought 3]

flip so many hats that i'm practically a hat rack /
stacked with so many personality shifts

that / you'll never know the really real one until
that hat lifts / you might catch a glimpse but

you'll have to second guess / coz the hat's coming
down / guess who's up next / could be

me at my best or the worst of the kids cursed to
make sense of men when pen pushing a

verse to quench thirst for consciousness shifting /
hat lifting / heads up / sucker the jigs

up / blind will find time to feel for the focus /
hopeless / unless you swop the hat for the

helmet / heaven seems cooler the hotter that
hell gets

the hats change but the head stays the same /
then the heart takes strain and the head

must change

straining like strings when the violin sings / bring
in a cello on a mellow for my type of

fellow / tell a whole lotta heads that wanna settle
for devils below the levels of bass

mentality / handing me heads with heavily
heavenly hats / selling me telling me I could

never be that / so why try crying high for the
crown of thorns when all you offer as

alternative's a head full of horns

the hats change but the head stays the same /
then the heart takes strain and the head

must change

148

I cap my crown with a cap not a crown
A king's just a kid who never felt the ground
underfoot / shoulda / stayed down with the
footmen
the foot not the crown gonna make the movement
we subject the king to grassroots objection
lifting collective heads we come and question:
pick another hat
which would he choose?
even far ahead it's still a head you could lose
save space for the meek in your majesty or you'll
be carrying your crown to the guillotine
x2
[break]

focussing on how I blast thoughts so my last thoughts are thoughts that last long beyond
body gone passed / focussing / I blast thoughts so my last thoughts are thoughts that last /
long beyond body gone passed...

1 and 2   3 and 4   1 and 2 and 3 and 4 and

BLUE LIGHT DROP

Get out the way y'all
Get out the way y'all
THE PRESIDENT just got dropped!
...OFF / at the palace / chilling in his chariot / sipping from his pimp cup / tinted windows all
up / AC blowing out a cool breeze exclusively flowing for these sweaty VIPs / while I get
squeezed out of my lane tryin ta maintain my own way my own direction / gotta make way
for the president's erection...
here come the cavalcade / blue light brigade /
haven't seen this parade since the days of Roman lanes when the Emperor was followed
by his freshest slaves while the people all showered him with popular praise /
Africa and Europe come from some similar days / making way for the presence of pride /
we swop the King's carriage out for a German ride / Mercedez amaze these / wonder
who's inside? / must be some big shots! / big enough to squeeze us aside on the way to
the top spots /
give 'em room / we can't make them late / VIP / got somewhere important to be / but it
doesn't matter how much room we make / the people on the other end still will wait /
for f*ck sakes / this is what it takes to be a Lord / be adored by the masses / you know

you've scored / when you can crush the crowd / push the people out the way / VIP all day singing TIA till it's judgement day...and the scales have to sway...till they tip on you fat cats...start to pray...

coz a ride ain't nothing but a throne on wheels / check it starts looking good for those who know no meals /

so now the poor man feels that he needs to own those wheels /

so he holds cold steel and steels his soul to steal /

but he'll never bust through the VIP protection so he aims at another brother from his section / he caps a connection coz hunger abounds / pounds the ground / feet meet street / running when the siren sounds /

now he's running for his life for his freedom to survive / he took another mans life / crime keeps him alive / so he's robbing and stealing like the leaders he knows / the only difference between them is the cut of their clothes /

coz orange or Armani a suit is still a suit / Selebi or Mdluli / poison root poison fruit /

so he's running from the sound of his heart beat drumming / the sound of the siren quickly coming / but it's not the cops / that's too much to ask / it's just another f*cking blue light going past...

Get out the way y'all

Get out the way y'all

THE PRESIDENT just got dropped!

...OFF / at the palace / chilling in his chariot / sipping from his pimp cup / tinted windows all up / AC blowing out a cool breeze exclusively flowing for these sweaty VIPs / while I get squeezed out of my lane tryin ta maintain my own way my own direction / gotta make way for the presidents erection...

I won't stand for the presence of the president / according to the party the President should stand for me / see these VIPs how they squeeze through the cities / pockets fat / skin thin / sleazy breed /

See I / see no need for the Blue Light goons / if they weren't so fat they wouldn't need all that room /

see they / freely consume all the space that it takes / putting belts on loose on an oversized waste /

see them / standing in line for a VIP ticket / bring that Blue Light / let me show you where to stick it...

Get out the way y'all

Get out the way y'all

THE PRESIDENT just got dropped!

Never called a MAN Boy
never called a WOMAN GIRL
all i'm saying i'm simply praying for a simple
world...

Never named another Nigga
Never called a cat Kaffir
See I always tried to keep my vocab bigger
See I believe the smaller the vocab
                the bigger the bigot
I maintain ~~there's~~ a million ways to say
                    "friggit"

"friggit" meaning "fu-getta-bout it"
say it how you want to
but depending on who hears you
don't say I ~~didn't~~ never warned you
See these words & will farm you
words used to frame you
the same way that same say that
    some words contain you

LIKE:
    I Never called a MAN BOY
    I Never called no woman Girl
    & i'm saying i'm simply praying for a
                            simple world

See, simply put, BOYS don't work in gardens, Men do,
coz sowing seeds, nurturing growth &
harvesting fruit is far too critical
a concern to leave to boys its true
                        ... MEN do.

LYING IRON ZION

When I think of ZION

I see no LION

I see them LYING

I see shackles of IRON

so I'm seeing "IRON / while they're LYING / about ZION"

Raise a fist against a ZIONIST who wanna teach a whole new lesson of what oppression is.

[Oops! Oops! Oops! Now they're upset. What did you expect? This is what I give because this is what I get. I get:]

"Have you BEEN to Israel?"

I say "No."

They say "Then what do you know?"

I say "What do I know?"

I say:

I know that not too long ago there was a night in Pretoria when the Jacarandas would

soon be in bloom, when you could listen to the song of a Night Jar,

while they bounced the brain and broke the body of Biko in the back of a cop car.

In 1960 I can say with certainty that someone was probably Braaing while in the dust of Sharpeville they lay dying.

I know that we were able to sing along "Be happy / Don't worry" while Madiba was going blind in a limestone quarry.

I haven't been, NO, and I don't WANT to go coz if I DO go, what will I see?

Tel Aviv University? Bastion of Middle Eastern Democracy?

Will I be allowed to see more? Maybe peek under the floor?

To dig a little deeper and discover the foundations, reveal the foundations,

the bones that those buildings are built on, Al-Shaykh Muwannis,

the old soil that blood was spilt on, Al-Shaykh Muwannis,

when they drove them in droves from their homes, from Al-Shaykh Muwannis, creating

plenty refugees,

but with ease they tell me that "This land was empty".

NO, I haven't been, and I WON'T GO,

coz Sprite got it half right:

Image IS nothing

Truth is everything

and showing my eyes lies would be as easy as pointing out how high your flag flies,

and while we watch it waving you can bulldoze and bury and cover with paving the spot where olive trees stood with fruit that was lush,

where Rachel Corrie stood before she was crushed,

before the bulldozer forever blended her body, her existence with the rubble of resistance.

I haven't been, NO, I WON'T GO, not till THEY check THESE points:

Not till the waters of the Gaza Strip are safe enough for children to sip;

Not till the wall comes down: between the crops and the town;

between the farmer and the fields;

between the stones and the steel;

between the gas and the mask;

between the victim and the blast;

Check THESE points and then maybe I will go and WHEN I go,

I will carry a picture of Hector Petersen,

to lay by the grave of Ehab Abu Nada, died September 2012, from self-immolation.

Think about him every time you light a fire,

remember how sometimes bodies seem to burn better then tires.

NO, I haven't been, I WON'T go, until Palestine is free.

When I think of ZION

I see no LION

I see them LYING

I see shackles of IRON

so I'm seeing "IRON / while they're LYING / about ZION".

Raise a fist against a ZIONIST who wanna teach a whole new lesson of what oppression is.

[Oops! Oops! Oops! Now they're upset. What did you expect? This is what I give because

this is what I get. I get:]

"Have you BEEN to Israel?"

I say "No."

They say "Then what do you know?"

I say "What do I know?"

I say nothing, because I know.

LUKA LESSON

Luke Haralampou, aka Luka Lesson, is a spoken word and Hip-hop artist of Greek heritage from Australia. With two years of international touring, eleven Writers' Festivals, seven years of workshop experience and almost ten years of writing under his belt, Luka has written commissions and performed for the likes of The Nuyorican Poets' Cafe (NYC), The National Gallery of Victoria, Trinity International Hip-hop Festival, Greece's pioneer Hip-hop group 'Active Member' and China's most celebrated living poet, Xi Chuan, in Beijing. He is also the Australian Poetry Slam champion of 2011 and Melbourne Overload Poetry Festival slam champion of 2010.

Academically Luka holds a first-class honours degree from Monash University and has taught side-by-side with Indigenous educators and staff at the Centre for Australian Indigenous Studies. He has co-ordinated and spoken at symposia relating to cross-cultural awareness and recently completed a Masters of Sound Design (Poetry Performance) through the Victorian College of the Arts. As a workshop facilitator Luka has assisted hundreds of people of all ages and backgrounds to write and perform their work, many for the first time.

CLOUDS FOR A TABLECLOTH

Freedom Charter signed the wrong dotted line
and collided with the sky

Freedom is still hungry

Truth still wearing a lie

Joy is almost superseded

They wonder if jagged edges solve purple hazes
when taken on the weekend

And deep vein gold mines

Eat them like mince

Biltong refugees spat out in a trench

I don't know shit

One month is not enough I busted up and rocked
some shows

Drank a little blood

Emancipated westerner

Still hanging in the shade

Almost got a tattoo too

But faded to avoid the lasers

I am a Tourist

I dove with the sharks

And ate on the table-top

Chomped a foot-hill of Pap

With clouds for a tablecloth

Gods for new friends genius discussions

Queens on pen and paper

Rushay is the King of introduction

And in the end it changed my life

It open chest surgeryed me

Closed the casket to my past

Medal of honour smokers

Two tokes from a Purple Heart

I saw the divide between the haves and the have-nots

Met Yeti Afrikaners with hairy hands

Sasquatch

Bought a meal for three dollars

And it made me look like I was rich

So I realized the privilege from being born
average when most of the world eats shit

And this is 'Africa Light'

She tells me with a smile

Million dollar mansions, barbed wire

And the lucky ones locked inside

And the anarchists heard me speak

The EFF said they're fans

So I understand how the vineyards in
Stellenbosch

Is where they should take back the land

And how being locked in a township means

You can't fight hand to hand

And being luckier than the last generation means
you're meant to treasure what you have

But that doesn't mean keeping silent and never
fighting for the next level

I'm just student in a classroom

In a country full of rebels

COINS OF LANGUAGE

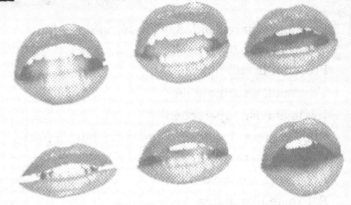

As coins fly over their heads like bats in summer
rivers swell to bursting as though the ground cries

cicadas warn the people of dangers
because nothing is more terrifying than to have your
language scraped from your lungs
and to be forced to use your oppressors' words
to articulate to them the depth of what they have
done

"Always was, always will be Aboriginal land"
could be translated into all of this nation's
indigenous languages
so it stays rooted in the earth
before histories haunt us like ghosts
but have no way to tell us who they are
before whole libraries commit suicide
and come back to tap us on the shoulder
but cannot tell us their names

language, a finite resource is
being extracted from
children like zinc
letters like shards of lead
words like gold
sentences of silver
paragraphs of iron ore
Dreaming story uranium
proverb purple oval

each lung a shaft

each rib a beam

more blood pumps new reserves

each vein a seam

each tongue a pick

each eureka a dream

each shovel a pencil

each stalactite a pen

each voice-pipe a tunnel

each truck a letter sent

each shipment a vocabulary

each elder a mountain

each son a new reserve

tears like diamonds

every lament a crack

every war-cry an explosion

each death another shaft collapsed

and while they sleep

coins fly over their heads like bats in summer

precious stones are sold and resold

and dug up and resold and dug up

and resold

and more cuts are opened up

and more cuts are resold and dug deeper

and resold and dug deeper

and cut up and opened and dug deeper

and shifted and sorted and melted down

and shipped to the port

and moored and measured and made clean

and moored and measured and made clean to be

placed in white frames and encased in a glass

placed in white frames and encased in a glass or
on white walls for the upper class

open cut mines pillaging raw lungs

the money pours through white pores

black tongues lick at the land like a slated lake

just to get a taste of their own dirt

and as they sleep

the coins fly over their heads like bats in summer

DEJAVU TAFARI

Kaleidoscopic display of
witty lyrics, ... characterisations and erratic
movement, Vuyokazi Ngemntu's
(aka Dejavu Tafari) poetic verse
is nothing if not eccentric. At best
a sincere attempt at social commentary
laced with a penchant for the fantastical,
what results is poetry which pushes the
boundaries of conventional writing and
'normal' thought patterns!

MY PECULIAR PRAISE SONG

A discordant gospel song lacking in the basic grace
of a soul that has just
chanced upon God's embrace
vomits its 59BPM affluence through my radio,
my bewilderment and discontent negotiating their immeasurable ratio
as I battle these lascivious urges – to no avail –
to pull the damn plug as though I were a toddler and it, a puppy's tail!
Heaven knows I need my fix of redemption.
Yes, I've been lobbying for God's immediate attention:
want Him comfortable in all his duality;
need Her non-elitist in her divine quality;
I want God flippin' a sixteen in tongues;
need Her pitching
freakin'
phly
high
notes
making other idols lose their votes,
exclaiming "damn, if I had her lungs!"
with a strength so fragile, it threatens never to break
but bends Him in all cardinal points
where marginal folks
still have offerings to make.

Miscarried (for Ngoma)

Dear child I will might will never know/
blao.
me a kiss from wherever you are/
you're far
Too much a part/
of the → hole in my heart
for me to forget/
How we almost met/
How you almost let/
me fall hopelessly in love with your eyes
and how your cries
al... woke me up at 4am/
cos you'd dreamt
that I was taken away from you/
on to
have dared to ponder/
your gender
and contemplate/
how to generate
enough

Burnt at the stake
for the sake of Her convictions;
succeeding to rise past His social conditions.
Tell God I need Her to hurry on up and slow down
coz there're too many teenage mothers in this damn town.
Tell Him his manhood is not beneath his belt but above his shoulders;
and that we'll continue to observe all the omens She showed us.

See, I don't want Him to think that I'm selfish
but could She magnify all the memories which I so relish,
like that of my father (Her son) beaming with pride at my achievements
and not so much that of my mother riddled with bereavement?

I'm ambivalent about this, but I want to need God,
though not the version that's got a blue-eyed son and carries an iron rod!
I need the grin of a toothless homeless man in response to a greeting;
kinda like the beat in my heart, worth repeating.
A constellation of ghetto superstars glowing… a celestial cipher.
The incantation song of high-tide waves that I long to decipher.
And if the radio at 4:34am must play so-called 'gospel'
Ask them to make this news so sexy, I could hear it in a brothel!

MISCARRIED
(FOR NGOMA)

Dear Child I Will Never Know,

blow

me a kiss from wherever you are.

You're far too much a part

of the hole in my heart

for me to forget

how we almost met.

How you almost let

me fall hopelessly in love with your eyes

and how your cries

almost woke me at 4am coz you dreamt I was
taken away from you.

Oh, to

have dared to ponder

your gender

and contemplate

how to generate

enough income

to make you think I'm

capable of giving you, my prince or princess
– and your three brothers

and two sisters – the world.

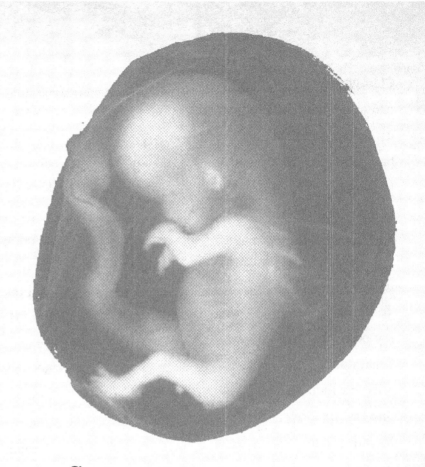

The hold

you have on my every other thought

every mother aught

to know is hard to relinquish,

for I little distinguish

between what is a dream

and what it may seem

is the grim

reality

that you shall not be.

See,

eight weeks of your
clandestine existence in my
womb had groomed me

to expect your imminent
presence in my room in the
next thirty-two.

Clearly you

can appreciate my predicament:

it's as if a ligament

has been torn from my soul.

My whole

being aches

and the whole thing makes

me demand answers to questions I cannot begin
to ask.

To mask

my pain,

I maintain

a logic which leans on pop psychology

and my apology

to your spirit

has in it

justifications

like "complications

in the first trimester

are a disaster

which are mostly unavoidable'".

The irreparable

damage

is one I manage

to pretend

to comprehend

through self-help manuals

and testimonials

like "How To Process Grief"

by some self-proclaimed 'doctor'

who's first chapter

reads nothing

like the cutting

scream

that seemed

stuck in my throat

when I ought

to have known

that the red river flowin'

from underneath my skirt

was in fact

you.

Do

tell me how I can write such a poem

as to make it known

that you drew

every ounce of my faith

and yet an eighth

when you disintegrated

shortly after you'd insinuated

yourself into my uterus.

Computerized

images generated from the first and only
sonogram leave me with less

than a hologram of your reflection.

Your retraction

from this world

is promptly told

in the faces of your siblings:

my evenings are spent piecing together their
features for each has me

confronting trace elements of a face adamant on
appearing in my dreams.

My whims

compel

me to tell

you that I WILL one day write you a poem that
will adequately and quite

eloquently say, "Ngoma, I hold you in my breath
and will search the earth

with all my heart for what words the gods will
instruct me to sing to bring

you to rest!"

Best

Wishes,

Your Mother still.

167

IN DEFENCE OF POETRY

I want to remind you that poetry isn't always written.

Twice shy, once bitten:

It's encoded in your body's memory,

Your eardrums when you hear the melody

Of a song you once danced to

By chance when your feelings asked you to!

Poetry is in the image of a casket descending to the grave;

In the rusty, broken chains of a medieval slave.

It's in the way your back arches to welcome a lover's embrace

Tracing its way from your spine to your face;

In how you react when your name is spoken

By someone with whom bonds were prematurely broken;

Like the poetic shuffle of insistent raindrops

Falling upon yielding corrugated iron rooftops.

You know how poetry sounds:

Soothing, caressing, injurious and debilitating,

At once both repulsive and scintillating.

Verses generously embossed on a page

Or violently thrust in the orifices of the psyche in rage.

It tastes like regret served in cold weather

With guilt and shame to garnish the platter.

Poetry is a virgin's first kiss – always stolen –

In autumn before the first leaf has fallen;

The rhythmic stomp of shamanic feet

And the chaos of traffic on a busy main street,

Home to none that traverse it,

A resource though none may possess it.

Belligerent, recalcitrant poetry!

Devotional, emotional poetry!

Erotic poetry! Repentant poetry!

Incriminating poetry, liberating poetry

Shouted through megaphones on the 30th floor of a dilapidated skyscraper

By a gang led by a stuttering catholic priest-turned-rapper;

By babies too bold to be born.

Poetry danced by an abuser's recently widowed punching bag, too relieved to mourn.

Poetry that reminds us that you can only have a standpoint

Once your throbbing feet have stood on the thorny mid-point

Between pro-life and pro-choice

And had circumstance dictate your voice

Away from the orchestra of religious doctrine

In response to a pain stronger than the effects of morphine;

Echoing at a place where you think God too loathsome to visit:

A part where your soul has the skin of a lizard:

Abrasive to love's touch

Though not dead as such.

Our poetry will remember to heal us.

Its words will burst from literature's cocoons and reveal us –

Primarily to our own selves –

And redeem us from our private hells!

From mothers whose despair can't stand sobriety

To young gay lovers excommunicated from Ghanaian society;

Fathers whose pride forbids them to seek forgiveness from their sons

And rape victims who've long swapped their pillows for guns.

Three year old girls whose ghosts must one day castrate their uncles

And big-boned girls who wear kaftans to hide their ankles

From a chorus which makes it fashionable for them to be deemed fat

And chemo patients who won't dare leave the house without a hat,

In fear of the ridicule and laughter

While walking past the corner of happy-ever-after:

Blonde little rich girls

Whose blue eyes colour their dark worlds

A vibrant chardonay hue,

Invisible but to the precious few

Who dwell in houses of glass

A stone throw from our Sharpeville past.

We whose spirits demand compensatory poetry,

Emergency sacrificial poetry,

Heal-each wound-one-by-one type poetry!

Don't forget-to-greet-the-Sun-type poetry!

Burn impepho and practise Kundalini-type poetry

Purge with muti then read the tarot-type poetry

Poetry to house our contradictions;

Poetry to challenge our strongest convictions.

Redemption poetry.

Condemnation poetry.

Loaded poetry for the empty spaces in our hearts.

Super-glue poetry for our spirits' broken parts.

We must have poetry!

DEAR SECRET LOVER

I don't expect you to love me silently
For I too would not know how to
respond quietly
To your collar-bone kisses
And gentle caresses.
This would be a waste of passion
Leading us both to question
Whether attraction is a crime.
So, Dear Secret Lover, let's rather
not waste our time.

Andrew is a writer, performance Poet, comedian and MC from Johannesburg. As a writer, he first came to prominence in 2010 when his submission for the University of Johannesburg International Students poetry competition emerged as the overall winner. Still a reluctant performer, it was not until 2011 that he committed to taking his art from page to stage. In that year he won the provincial leg of the Drama for Life Poetry Challenge (Gauteng) & took second place in the hotly contested National Grand Slam of the same competition. In November of 2011 he took 3rd place at the Word N Sound Poetry Festival Open Mic Finale and has been extensively involved in Word N Sound throughout 2012, wherein he once again placed in the top 5 of their Open Mic League. As a writer he has edited the AFM magazine "This is My Story", and has worked as an assistant-editor for the Christian book "Spiritual Confessions for Various Situations" authored by Pastor Kundai Matope. The peculiar mix of comedy and poetry that Andrew has been able to combine, has also allowed him to bring a fresh perspective to MC-ing. Being a born-again Christian, he strives to represent Christ through his art. He is the holder of BCom Marketing Management & BCom (Hons)Strategic Management degrees and is an emerging entrepreneur.

ANDREW MANYIKA

PROMISES & SECRETS

I finally made it to the mouth of the river that feeds
the endless stream of sweet nothings that only lovers
channel.

And as I sat upon its banks, I drew the tears from my
eyes and as they met with its waters, I knew then why
this river, always honeysweet in its beginnings, runs
bittersweet before the last sip.

A Good Book I read once told me, "A three-strand cord
is not easily broken"
(that is the problem).

A bad life I lived once showed me "A secret kept
between three is too easily spoken"

And when that silence is taken as a token, that trust as
a bond remains unbroken,

It leaves one unaware and unprepared

for the slap of reality by which one will be woken.

SHHHH

There's a discomfort about silent houses;
About walking in halls where sound should be
And finding that it isn't.
An empty house is nothing to go back to.
It's not like a 3am traffic light
Relaying its message even if there is
No one to listen.
An empty house is a great gutted thing, a stuffed beast
Filled with memories mocked by eerie silences
And the spaces in between them, that will often reveal
to you
A stranger: you.
A strangeness brought on because at the end of the day,
At the beginning of it and in all the hours in between,
All there is, is you.

You pause in between bouts of stealing the sounds of
your neighbours,
Aware of having become a stranger to yourself.
Is the silence the absence of something missed?
Or the presence of a stifling something in the corners,
Something that hissed?

TRAJECTORY OF A TEAR by

Reading,
Of emotions, tugging at the heart
Bringing curiosity to the things
Open eyes, slipped beams
of light, into the tearduct, or
with gears stuck, ascends a
toward the solitary top.

As it is battling, through th
Einddling, this fore line a
to ascend against gravity
of the syphon in the du
but doesn't violently e

But on reaching the p
keepin' them open, p
as it looks closer
Then it's downhill

Sliving slipper
becoming des
ember me, b
of each pe
When it is ca

174

There's a disquietude about silent people,
They bring it with them, the silence,
But forget to take it with them when they go.
They harbour things within them
Like ships in a port.
And struggling under the waves of a tide that doesn't
break,
They take upon themselves
The burden of things that cannot be spoken
Because they never learned and were never taught
How to speak to a world that answers
Before it has taken the time to hear the questions.

The quiet they carry runs deeper than stagnant
waters,
And it can drown you,
And leave you bathing in the uncomfortable
things, thinking:
Sound should be here.
Now I've stood in that silence,
I've swam against that current,
And those silences were never awkward,
But God knows they were never easy.

175

An Hourglass!
A Pair of Wayfarers!
A Chalice!

Hold the image, as the tale of the untold damage
Done to a wax-winged bird, bold in plumage, unfolds.
She plummets as she drifts on the ocean,
Tossed here by the winds of reason,
There by the waves of emotion.
She tweets to no avail,
Tries to speak, but does not prevail.
And as the tide breaks, she washes ashore,
Beached without a sail.

We don't outgrow needing to be touched.
And she had never needed it as much as she did,
Waiting on the silent sound to tell her she could fly again.
She lay on the sand and made a mattress of the grains,
And as the hours passed, she stands at last
And shakes those grains into her hourglass.
She turns it.
This is how her time amongst us begins.
She forsakes the form of the creature with broken wings,

The bird has blossomed and become human,
Better yet, she has chosen the way fairer form
And become, a woman.
In the meantime, I put on my wayfarers, and step to the stage
Because I am a rapper and I spit with rage.
I scream and say, "I'm ill! & can only get iller.
Ladies know love doesn't get much realer
Than in the arms of a legitimate lady-killer.
I'm like a lion in wait but I pounce like Godzilla!"
As I step off stage something brings her to my field of vision.
As we speak it clicks that she's here because she followed the links to my site.
I proceed to bind her to myself with a chain of links to my sight.
I take off my glasses and let her in – the hourglass turns.
This is how our time together begins.

Months pass and as we stand after I've caught her,
It strikes me how she is like a lamb to the slaughter,
A sheep in the big city, or as she puts it, 'pig city'.
We're stagnant, static, but the electricity activates her sexually,

And with my wayfarers on I try to sell myself this illusion,

That the way is fairer on a road with me, but I'm disillusioned

Because love or piety won't let me be a Pharisee

And given how far I see,

I acknowledge the truth and abandon the player's doctrine

And without getting a doctor in

I diagnose her heart's condition – in love.

I try to stop her before she starts the mission but I'm late,

So before this becomes the tale of a tragic blossom,

I pull her aside and try to explain to her that dammit

Due to the former exploits of what I thought was my "magic" Johnson,

I'm ill, and I can only get iller.

And, yes, I know, love doesn't get much realer

But if you choose me you make me a literal lady-killer.

What's eating at me is lying in wait,

And I'll pounce on you like Godzilla.

But it's like she's not listening.

It's like she's playing at picking Pokémon, pointing her finger at me and saying,

"Godzilla! I choose you."

The paradox of the innocent bystander

Is that there is no innocence in standing by.

So I'm guilty of not driving home the point

That because of what we've done,

We're warming ourselves with fires from the cool side of the sun.

We're still burning, and that's a truth she knows so her eyes are churning.

I try to trace the trajectory of her tears but lose my way

Because they're lost in the laughter lines still lingering round her lips.

Yes, she's smiling.

We don't outgrow wanting to be touched.

What we don't choose, is by whom, where and how much.

I touched her heart and it splintered.

She takes two shards.

With the first she clips her own wings and becomes earthbound

And abandons making bird sound.

With the second she cuts a hole in the hourglass and turns it,

And we watch our time running out.

Finally empty, the hourglass becomes our glass, a chalice

From which we both take sips.

It's an act of love done without malice.

But as we sip the contents,

Dreams of the future, are born, dance and die

In the mingling of our now mangled lips.

Thabiso Mohare (also known as Afurakan) is one of the pioneers behind Johannesburg's underground Spoken Word scene. He is best known for his stage improvisations on hip-hop tunes. His style has caught the attention of many poets and writers across Africa and the world with its rhythm and provocative nature. His activity within Jozi's poetry movement can be traced back to the "So where to" poetry events, and his work with the poetry collective Soul 2 Mouth, among others. Afurakan has played a vital role in the growth of the spoken word movement in Johannesburg and indeed South Africa; and he's a regular at schools and community centres, performing for the purpose of spreading the word. He is the co-founder of Word N Sound Poetry & Live Music Series – a ground breaking poetry development project that has been running in Johannesburg since 2010. www.wordnsound.wordpress.com

Performances highlights: Africa Cup Of Nations 2013 Opening ceremony, London Olympics 2012, Arts Alive 2012, Shoko Festival 2012 - Zimbabwe, Macufe 2012, SANAA African Festival 2012, World Festival of Black Arts 2010 - Senegal.

AFURAKAN

WHERE WERE YOU?

Where were you when the revolution was sold for a tender belly?

When the children were fed snake and stone instead of fish and bread!

Where were you when technicolor dreams of freedom woke up to an animal farm?

A sun scorched reality of haves and have-nots,

Poisoned soil makes waste of the farmer's time and toil.

What harvest shall come from these young and fertile minds?

Where were you when we watched the revolution televised?

Still waiting for change and a better life.

Where were you when they ate cake and toasted on your behalf?

Dined on your budget and gave a hearty laugh.

Where were you when he danced?

Will do anything but deliver on the promise so he danced.

As though dancing for his life.

He danced.

And sang with a smile.

He danced.

Where were you when the revolution shot 36?

Capitalist guns know no bounds.

Where were you when minimum wage cost a human life?

They keep robbing the earth.

How many lives for an ounce?

Where were you when townships burned?

A page out of history, haven't we learned?

Where were you when bullets and stones crossed paths?

Blood can be washed off but the memory lasts.

Where were you when we drove in coffins on highways of dreams?

Where were you when we shacked survival in tin boxes hoping to mute its screams?

Where were you when a black man was president?

Where were you when the revolution was a tender document?

ANTHEM FOR DOOMED POETS

21-poem salute

For the writer who died on stage thinking his ego is word-proof

Your technique is not unique

Your blackberry tweet is not a haiku

Your facebook book status not a poem

Your blog is not a novel

Nothing epic

You need to read more

Let knowledge unveil your ignorance

Maybe you can see more

And be more

Informed

Before you throw careless speech

At a time when men and women die for the words they speak.

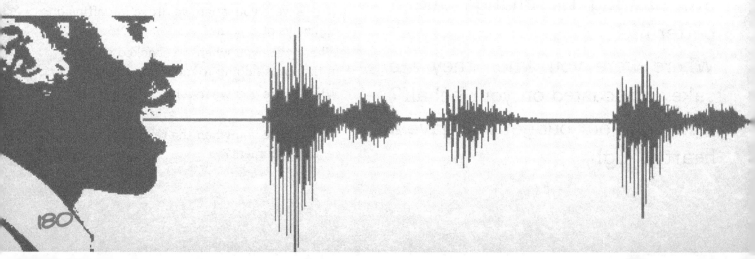

A BLUES FOR MADIBA

The fathers of our nation
Have made wives and concubines of our daughters
With liquor stained breath
They drive lies
Big as mines
Discarding family lives
Just to park their success
Between varsity thighs

A social degree in networking
Flash cash to hungry eyes
A gold card can hypnotize
The morning after is not important

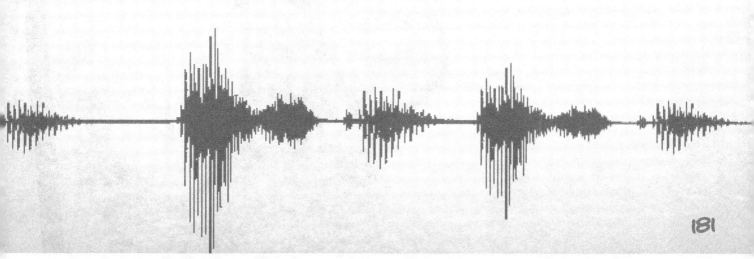

MANDI POEFFICIENT VUNDLA

Mandi Poefficient Vundla is a writer
and spoken word ambassador who hails
from Soweto. She made her debut
in the world of competitive poetry
in 2011. Dubbed Queen of the Mic
after defending her Word N Sound
Title not once but twice!!

MUSICAL NOTE TO KWAITO

Some songs sound like suicide notes
rattling from skeletal bones
walking falsetto drones through the high
pitched struggle of the ghetto.
A requiem for Soweto,
where artists raise hope like crescendos
from spirits living at their lowest keys
inaudible hymns breath in
a cappella heartbeats
pumping the rendition of a broken pulse
dumped in the chorus of the slums
we run like cassettes from substations
playing our own tracks with vibrato in the backyard
houses shaken from their skulls by the rhythm
in the background.
We sound like a key to broken backroom ballad
in the classical struggle kwaito never fails to sing.
A genre built from informal settling beats
that stand like a bridge in the township
where we cross our fingers around musical hearts

that Zola is no demon
possessed by the slums
composing hit tracks to beat on his women.
That he doesn't conduct his quartet of children
with the same strings he pulls to swear at woman
like Mpho.
Mandoza's broken record
is recovering from a stroke
that left her as broken as his English
as frail as his body language
the anguish on his face
is a music compilation of mistakes
that reminds me of Zombo's solo fallen weight.
A fully blown trumpet of aids
blowing it's last regret
over our heads
so we question the music we play into our beds
umthandazo wabo lova
couldn't save Brown Dash
from dying with nothing in his hands.

The gap between his teeth
opened like a mass grave
lowering his body in volume
to rest underground music
his bones lay
6 feet deeper than the baritone
humming him down an orchestra of death
reminding me of when
Spiki-riki-wiki wept saying "Kuyafana, we're all
gonna die someday."
Makes me wonder what monsters get produced
with these tracks.
Somebody tell Mshoza to bring the heartbeat black
bleach can't fade the colour of your lineage,
the way your ebony arms dance around the word piti
we should call it pitty
how black breaths fade on air
from stagelights to the grave sites
they puff and pass on to the other side.
They hang their boots with their mics
laced with starving chords beneath their tongues
some found food for the soul beneath the basslines,
rose like soprano above the breadline
from tunes left behind in their breadcrumbs.

They sampled the sound of their grumbling
stomachs
into double platinum albums
but when they top the charts
these double platinum stars drop
into the dusty streets they came from.

When a good example rots in a chorus behind
bars
bricks holding cells up
from bodies crumbling down
twinkle twinkle Ndikhokhele fallen star
how I wonder where your songs are

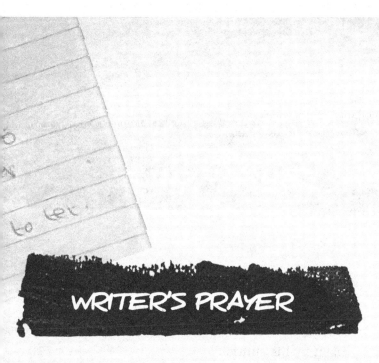

WRITER'S PRAYER

This is to all the revolutionary writers I know
the ones who make nouns sound like verbs
you are doing words right.
with body parts of speech
your gestures move in linguistics
you cross your legs in cursive
you sit like cliché
you stand like a pen clicking it's tongue across the stage
as blunt as pencil
sharpened too many lives but still remain broken
into pieces of chalk
surrounding your heart like classrooms walls
in the school of an audience
anxious at their desks
for the chapters in your breaths
to snap their fingers out of apathy.

Hug them like calligraphy
curling its arms around people to read them in stanzas
from poems you've written in genres of speech.
Building communities in sonnets
takes over 14 horizons
when your 15th line
still hasn't saved a child
you feel like a helpless lifeguard
watching your inner man drown his sorrows in ink
for the whole world to read
your body like script
moves like pages vigorously flipped
your pulse beats the time bombs were meant to tick coz you're explosives
your names are riots of alphabets
hiding armies beneath your accents
you're rolling your tongues into AK47's
you're smuggling guns in your grammar
typing bullets in your notes to shoot straight to the point
we're growing old
our history is ageing
the timelines have wrinkled into fiction
but it's up to you
to keep the truth young in its youth

Salute

SOME MEN WEAR DEADLY SMILES

Some men wear deadly smiles
that stretch as far as the crucifix
so they nail you to their deepest desires
hang you like a portrait at the cross of their fingers.

He will hold you in the frame of his breath
inhale you from the lens of his spectacles
as he preys on the temple of your body
like it is 80% holy water.

You will drizzle him from your blessed heavens
whilst he carves you into his inner art of sin
this masterpiece of want
his eyes opened like a gallery of lust.
The paintings on the windows of his soul
hung like a dry joke cracking through my aching
dawn
we spoke with my gasping stroke of ink.
Dripping from the wee hours of wind was the
sound of my breaking.

When the day breaks it down
I become enlightened by the sun
my hopes
risen by his sunrise
my horizon met with his eye line
and settled like dust in the dusk
of his full moon hugs where the stars gazed at
our spark from his pallet of sky.

I eclipsed in his crescent arms
clenched in the night of his lunar heart
draped in his expanse of skin.

Earth bound me to him
this son of a planet
orbiting mixed zodiac feelings
made me leap like a year of faith
to his soul a system that failed me.

His constellation of meteor lies began to glow
from his dark side
But i still think the world of this night and
shining demon
his eyes are shaped like the whole of China
getting smaller by the continent
his lips opened from the borderlines of longing
to gulp me home to the thirst of his body
where I searched for his inner most core
to quench my trembling soul.

When he spoke it was like he was matching
words from his closet
whilst packing me up for a storm.
The Ozone layered me with warmth
it knows love can forecast natural disasters.

The wind mills should have warned me
that cyclones come dressed as God-fearing men
who pin respect to the cloth of lingering air
tailor made from a two faced season of praise.

He was as tall as my shortcomings
as handsome as a beautiful verse on a down-
trodden soul.
He stood like a church bent in all night prayer
from a book where i had kept myself unread
for him.

In a poem like this.

Printed in the United States
By Bookmasters